JOURNEYS T
BRIGANTIA

JOHN DIXON
AND
PHILLIP DIXON

VOLUME ONE:

Walks in Craven, Airedale and Wharfedale

JOURNEYS THROUGH BRIGANTIA
VOLUME ONE:
CRAVEN, AIREDALE & WHARFEDALE

By

John Dixon & Phillip Dixon

Copyright © John Dixon & Phillip Dixon 1990

Published by Aussteiger Publications,
8 Back Skipton Road, Barnoldswick BB8 5NE.
Tel. (0282) 812741

Typeset by:
Hargreaves Steel Limited,
133 Henry Street, Church, Accrington, Lancashire BB5 4EP

Printed by:
Lamberts of Settle

First edition, July 1990

ISBN 1 872764 01 0

The sketch maps in this book are intended to indicate the route in a general way. Walkers should use Ordnance Survey Pathfinder maps to locate exact routes.

Whilst all the walks use established and definitive footpaths, walkers are requested to respect the privacy of residents and not to stray from the footpaths.

Please observe the Country Code.

Dedicated to Jaana

AUSSTEIGER PUBLICATIONS

Contents

JOURNEYS THROUGH BRIGANTIA

VOLUME ONE:
Craven, Airedale & Wharfedale

VOLUME TWO:
Ribblesdale, Malham & Central Wharfedale

VOLUME THREE:
Lower Wharfedale, Wasburndale & Ilkley Moor

VOLUME FOUR:
Upper Ribblesdale, The Three Peaks
& Upper Wharfedale

VOLUME FIVE:
Nidderdale, Knaresborough & Wensleydale

VOLUME SIX:
Swaledale, Teesdale & the Vale of Eden

VOLUME SEVEN:
The Lune Valley & Forest of Bowland

A Lakeland series will be entitled

JOURNEYS INTO RHEGED

Introduction

The books in this series are not intended for the 'plod-on-Larry' type of walker but for the more discerning and adroit wanderer who requires a meaningful exploration of the landscape, returning with a fuller appreciation of the environments they have ventured into.

The walks undertaken take on the nature of a journey through a bygone world, being the central areas of a once tribal zone known as Brigantia. For the most part centred on the Yorkshire Dales, an area of outstanding natural beauty and historical heritage.

We shall follow a Celtic peoples as they emerge in the dawn of Northern history to become the most famed of British tribes to resist the might of Rome, and their emergence from that period only to face further struggles from European incomers, the stories of which have come down to us in Arthurian legend.

Fortunately other sources exist for us to gain a truer picture of those times. The disciplines of Archaeology, Architecture, Philology and History are brought together for this reconstruction and presented here in a format that all can understand and gain from.

The walks themselves stand in their own right and take the reader-cum-explorer through the finest and most diverse countryside that can be found outside the Lakes in England. Great care has been taken to check out all the walking instructions, and for this service we thank all those too numerous to mention here. Thank you all.

J. L. & P. G. Dixon.

I first started to work on this series of books in the spring of 1988 with my then colleague, the Finnish artist Jaana Järvinen. Her death in October 1988 was a sad blow to myself and her family. Some of the last line drawings she worked on are included in this book. Jaana is dearly missed, but her inspiration and memory live on — John Dixon.

HISTORICAL BACKGROUND

The authors' intentions when embarking on the production of the 'Journeys through Brigantia' series are to provide concise field guides to the archaeology of the North of England. The walks described herewith will provide the reader with an insight into the interaction of man and the environment through the ages.

The walks explore some of the finest upland country in Britain; thus within a short distance of industrial conurbations the reader can escape to a most beautiful landscape rich in historical heritage.

It will become apparent that the authors' prime interest is in the history of the north in pre-feudal times. This does not mean that the authors ignore the area's rich heritage of mediaeval, religious and secular architecture. The Pennine hills could not be adequately explored without reference to the many sites which attest to the key role these regions played in early industrial development.

The authors are firm in their belief that not only does man shape his environment, but the environment is a major influence in the affairs of men. Ancient society can be divided into three types: urban, pastoral and arable. The existence of the urban environment is dependent on the surplus products of an arable hinterland. The population in an arable community tend to be closely tied to the soil which grows their basic food and economic unit — grain. Because corns need to be tended on a three season cycle, men who live by tending crops are not mobile and therefore more likely to be subject to political, economic and social domination.

The nature of pastoral farming in marginal upland areas tends to produce a semi nomadic society. In the winter flocks and herds have to be brought down to the valley bottoms to overwinter. In late spring after lambing sheep and cattle would be driven back to the summer pastures high on the fells. The valley bottoms now free from stock could be left to grow hay for winter fodder. The semi nomadic peoples of Eurasia have many traits in common. They tend to be fiercely independent and warlike. Many features of society in the Highlands of Caledonia, Hibernia, Celtic Gaul and ancient Greece can be mirrored in the pastoral peoples of central Asia. The Hun, Goth, Maggar, Kurd and Mongol needed his horse and weapons to defend his herds and flocks. When grazing failed, the herds and people had to move in search of new lands.

The history of Europe in ancient times is the story of the conflict between waves of peoples from the East aggressively probing at the frontiers of the Roman and Byzantine world. Before the coming of Roman rule virile pastoral societies existed in north western Europe. In the region covered by this series of books the most powerful kingdom in ancient Britain held sway — the Kingdom of Brigantia.

Brigantia was a typical pastoral society with its family and clan structure. The high kings of Brigantia probably had their religious and political 'foci' in the western vale of York and vale of Mowbray. In Roman times the client administration of Brigantia was based on Aldborough near Boroughbridge — just across the river from a vast complex of Iron Age and Bronze Age religious sites which are found between the Swale and Ure. Further north was the vast Brigantian oppidum at Stanwick — which control the frontier region between the vale of Mowbray and the once rich farmlands of south Durham, now covered by the Teesside conurbation.

The rugged geography of the north dictated that political power had to be devolved via the clan (sub-tribe) system to local strongmen (sub-kings). The Brigantian Kingdom stretched from sea to sea from the Tweed in the north to the dales of Derbyshire. Within this region only the Parisi people of east Yorkshire maintained their independence. Within Brigantia only a handful of the sub-clans have been identified. On the Lancashire coast the Setantii dominated. In the vale of Eden the Carvetii clan were granted a degree of local autonomy by imperial Rome.

With the collapse of Roman power in the fifth century, the Celtic structure of society re-emerged. The political unity of the north was broken and a host of Anglian and Celtic (British) kingdoms emerged. One of these post Roman Celtic Kingdoms spanned upper Wharfedale, Ribblesdale and Airedale — the Cantrev (kingdom) of Craven.

As Roman central political power dissolved in the early fifth century the native population returned to living in semi-defended farmsteads which like Bomber Camp (encountered on Walk 2, Vol.1) shows signs of society still trying to cling on to aspects of Roman culture. The history of these farmstead dwellers is not recorded in the conventional sense. History of ancient times

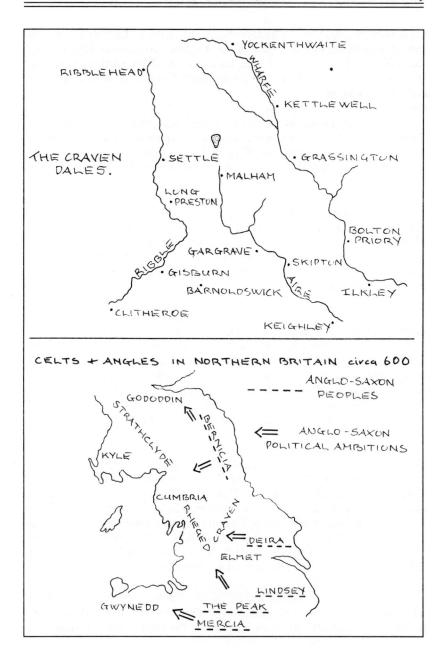

THE CRAVEN DALES.

RIBBLEHEAD
YOCKENTHWAITE
WHARFE
KETTLEWELL
GRASSINGTON
SETTLE
MALHAM
LONG PRESTON
BOLTON PRIORY
RIBBLE
GARGRAVE
SKIPTON
GISBURN
AIRE
ILKLEY
BARNOLDSWICK
CLITHEROE
KEIGHLEY

CELTS + ANGLES IN NORTHERN BRITAIN circa 600

ANGLO-SAXON PEOPLES

ANGLO-SAXON POLITICAL AMBITIONS

GODODDIN
STRATHCLYDE
BERNICIA
KYLE
CUMBRIA
RHEGED
CRAVEN
DEIRA
ELMET
LINDSEY
GWYNEDD
THE PEAK
MERCIA

tends to be recorded by the victors. Bede, the father of English history, recorded in some detail the origins of the Anglian Kingdoms of Bernicia and Deira. However, our sources for the history of the Celtic northern kingdoms are a few references in Bede, the Anglo-Saxon Chronicles and a handful of early Welsh sources.

The only conventional evidence for the existence of the Celtic Kingdom of Elmet in lower Airedale is a brief note that in 616 Ethelfrid of Northumbria drove out Cerdic, the last Celtic King of Elmet. However the extent of this kingdom can be judged by over 20 place-names which where described as 'in Elmet' in mediaeval sources.

At the time of the Norman Survey the settlements in the north west corner of the West Riding of Yorkshire are described as 'in Craven'. The origin of the place-name 'craven' is Celtic from the common root as the Gaelic for garlic — hence the land of garlic. In former times the heavily wooded banks of the Wharfe, Aire and Ribble would have been characterised in early summer by the scent of wild garlic.

In these 'Journeys through Brigantia' we shall visit the sites which provide evidence of the first humans to visit this region — the primitive hunter-gatherers who sheltered in Victoria Cave above Settle (Walk 4, Vol.2). The first recognisable society which existed in the Pennines were a Bronze Age people who buried the cremated remains of their aristocracy in urns in barrows and cairns (Walks 4 & 8, Vol.1, Walks 2 & 5, Vol.2). Evidence for their complex religious beliefs are revealed among the stone circles and mysterious cup and ring marked rocks high on Ilkley Moor (Walk 7, Vol.1).

It was from these people that the Iron Age society of Brigantia emerged. At Grassington (Walk 6, Vol.2) we shall walk among their settlements and field systems of well over 2,000 years ago. The stone severed heads at Coniston Cold and the Sha-na-gig figure at Hellifield (Walk 2, Vol.2) testify to the druidic religion found on the eve of the Roman conquest. The Romans found it necessary to build their forts in Craven to control their Celtic subjects: at Long Preston (Walk 2, Vol.2), Elslack (Walk 9, Vol.1) and Malham Moor (Walk 7, Vol.2). At Gargrave (Walk 5, Vol.1) stood a sophisticated Roman Villa — probably built for a Romanised Celtic landowner.

The religion of the earliest society in the Pennines was the urn culture which persisted for over a thousand years. The 'urn and circle' culture seems to have developed into the Iron Age cult of the severed head. Overlaid on these native influences were the diety religions of ancient Rome and the Middle East. By the sixth century A.D. one semitic belief had established its supremacy — the cult of the man-god who defeated death by resurrection.

The Celtic people of Craven and its sister states probably embraced Christianity from the fifth century onwards. Their Christianity developed in isolation from Papal authority. The pagan beliefs of the Angles of east Yorkshire added a religious division to the already existing linguistic and racial divisions. The conversion of Edwin of Northumbria seems to have been the precondition of his great political achievement — the unification of the north under the Northumbrian Kingdom. The remains of the high crosses at Addingham, Ilkley and Gargrave mark the advance of Roman Christianity and Anglo-Saxon power into the hinterland of the Pennines.

The 'ton' and 'ham' place-names of Craven reflect the replacement of the Celtic language by a Germanic tongue. In the high reaches of the Dales the semi-nomadic existence of former times persisted. In the more gentle landscape south-east of Gisburn can be found a village probably founded by Anglian settlers during this time (Walk 2, Vol.1).

To a large extent geographical factors defined patterns of settlement in Craven. The high dales could only support isolated farmsteads. In the lower lying areas are small villages, or rather hamlets, often no more than a cluster of farmsteads. The main settlements of Craven tend to be in the Aire valley, close to the rich arable riverside pastures and townfields.

From the highest point of navigation in ancient times on the Wharfe (Tadcaster) a chain of ancient riverside settlements linked the river system of the Humber basin — up into Craven and westwards towards the Ribble valley and the Irish Sea (Rombalds Way). A secondary trade route ran north west out of Craven towards Cumbria and Scotland.

It was this route which was used by Catroe on his epic tenth century pilgrimage from Fife to Gaul. Catroe and twelve companions were given safe passage from the borders of Fife by Donald King of the Strathclyde Britons, down into his sub-kingdom of Cumbria with its capital at Carlisle. Catroe probably moved south to the Anglian monastery at Heversham on Morecambe Bay and then turned south east to follow what is today the A65 into the heart of Craven and the Archbishop's residence at Addingham.

We are told that King Donald's bodyguards conducted Catroe to Leeds where he was left in the protection of Gunderic, an English noble. Gunderic then rode with Catroe to York and presented him at the court of Eric Bloodaxe.

The sight of warriors and pilgrims on the ancient routes of Craven would have been common. In winter the Aire Gap is the safest trans-Pennine route even in the age of the motorway. Throughout history people and products have passed this way. In the Bronze Age Irish gold and Lakeland axes, in the Iron Age salt, metal traders and slaves. The Roman garrisons of Lancashire and the Lake District would have been supplied from depots in the arable Vale of York, and the Aire Gap would have been a strategic point on the supply line.

In Anglo-Saxon and Viking times political dominance of the western Pennines was dependent on the control of the Aire Gap, Stanegate and Stainmore trade routes. It is no coincidence that in Feudal times Skipton Castle was built to control the Aire Gap of Craven.

The Norman Conquest of England had a revolutionary effect on the former kingdom of Northumbria. The Norman King decided to solve the problem of the unruly mixed British, Norse, Danish and Anglo-Saxon population by a policy of genocide. Most of Yorkshire was wasted — an act of barbarism ranking only with the genocides of this century of the Armenians, Kurds, European Jews, South American Indians and the San peoples of South Africa.

The generation that succeeded the pious Duke William of Normandy were forced with land holding with sparse populations and therefore of little value. Vast tracts of land were given over to Forest for game hunting; also, massive areas were given over to the newly established monastic houses. The peasant population now recovering from the Norman genocide now faced a new threat — eviction to make way for sheep ranches.

The vast monastic complexes of Fountains Abbey and Bolton Priory which once dominated the economy of Craven were built on a ruthless exploitation of land and men. The establishment of the monastic mono economy held back the social and economic development of the Dales for over 300 years. The break up of the Monastic estates was the stimulus for the rapid economic development that paved the way for the Industrial Revolution. This latter development is outside the scope of the present study.

THE CELTIC AGE
A return to tribalism

As the Roman control of Britain fell into a state of diminution many independent British kingdoms emerged throughout much of the country. These were probably deliberately established by the Roman administration in its last years and based on the local nobility. Alternatively the last of the Roman military commanders may simply have continued to wield effective power with whatever military forces remained at their disposal after the links with Rome had been broken, so that the dynasties which they established became the ruling houses of the later period.

Honorius' official answer to the cities of Britain telling them to look to their own defences, apparently in reply to a request for assistance, should be interpreted as giving official permission to the cities to act independently of the central government in recruiting and paying troops for their defence, thus legal sanction was given to the independence of the cities and by implication to their new rulers also.

The Roman administrative system was based on the division of the countryside between a number of civitates, whose curia was responsible for the administration of their own area. In the later Empire the responsibility for local military defence also rested on their shoulders. This curial class was composed of the local noble families, one of whom might be more prominent and influential than the others and so act as the military commander of an area — as was the case in pre-Roman times with the Brigantian confederacy.

The withdrawal of imperial government in 410 meant that those holding power locally had to take over the executive power completely. From the genealogies of the British kings of the North it would seem that the founders of the dynasties were established in power sometime in the latter part of the fourth century or the first part of the fifth.

In this early period Coel Hen and Dyfnwal Hen established their sway over major areas of territory in North Britain, the peoples of which were known as 'Gwyr y Gogledd' — Men of the North. Cunedda established his rule over North Wales and maintained close relations with his northern neighbours. All the kings of the sixth century British kingdoms traced their ancestry back to a very small group of men, suggesting that the main kingdoms established in the early period were subdivided amongst the sons of the founders to make more manageable units, while in some cases there were subordinate kings ruling smaller areas within the main kingdoms. Gargrave was possibly the centre of such a kingdom based on Craven.

The territories of the kingdoms which emerged after the sub-divisions were very similar to those of the Iron Age kingdoms of the pre-Roman period. This may have been partly determined by geographical considerations but the survival of British regional names suggests that some at least of the kingdoms may have been based on the major Roman administrative areas which were themselves derived from the Iron Age pattern.

The early British kingdoms are distinguished by a number of similar characteristics and principles that apply to all the early Welsh hundreds. Firstly, among the Welsh, as among other Indo-European peoples, the primary political unit, one ruled by a petty king, was often no larger than a mediaeval hundred. Secondly, the seat of government/court in any unit of administration would be in the subdivision of the 'hundred' being an important natural boundary, such as a river or wood.

These subdivisions or commotes would be further subdivided, the characteristic subdivision being a multiple estate containing a number of significant settlements determined by the quality of land in the cantrev; some would have greater multiples of land if the land quality was poor, others fewer if the land quality was good.

According to a relatively late Venedotian 'model' there were in every cantrev (hundred) two commotes each of fifty vills. The latter were grouped into twelve multiple estates each of four vills. The two vills that remained out of the hypothetical fifty were royal units. One, usually in the lowlands, contained the royal caput, the mensal/demesne land for the sustenance of the court, and an adjacent reeve's settlement. The second, usually in the uplands, was to be the king's waste and summer pasture. Monastic communities and churches featured at this time and it is known that church and court stood together at the administrative core of the cantrev/hundred.

Thirdly, characteristic of the more important Welsh multiple estates would be a large hill-fort which though first constructed in the Iron Age, could well have continued to serve as the retreat for the local community in times of conflict. Finally, the most important churches of all, and certainly those which later developed into diocesan seats, were located on the borders between commotes at the administrative cores of the hundreds.

In this and other volumes we shall attempt to unravel the present settlement patterns, based on Scandinavian and later Norman institutions, and rediscover the Celtic realms of the North, those lands once ruled over by the Dynasty of Coel Hen.

BLOODLINES OF THE NORTH BRITISH KINGS

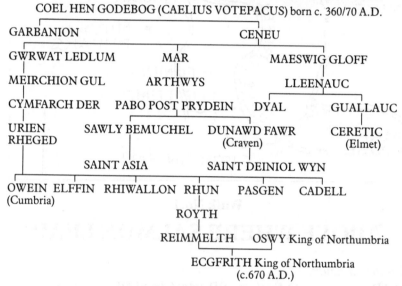

COEL HEN GODEBOG (CAELIUS VOTEPACUS) born c. 360/70 A.D.

GARBANION   CENEU

GWRWAT LEDLUM   MAR   MAESWIG GLOFF

MEIRCHION GUL   ARTHWYS   LLEENAUC

CYMFARCH DER   PABO POST PRYDEIN   DYAL   GUALLAUC

URIEN   SAWLY BEMUCHEL   DUNAWD FAWR   CERETIC
RHEGED   (Craven)   (Elmet)

SAINT ASIA   SAINT DEINIOL WYN

OWEIN ELFFIN RHIWALLON RHUN   PASGEN   CADELL
(Cumbria)

ROYTH

REIMMELTH   OSWY King of Northumbria

ECGFRITH King of Northumbria
(c.670 A.D.)

In future Volumes we shall try and place these kings in context, examine their rivalries and conflicts between themselves and the Anglian newcomers. We shall continue the Historical Background with the rise of Northumbria and the later Scandinavian immigrations, and then go on to look at the Norman period and its legacy to the North.

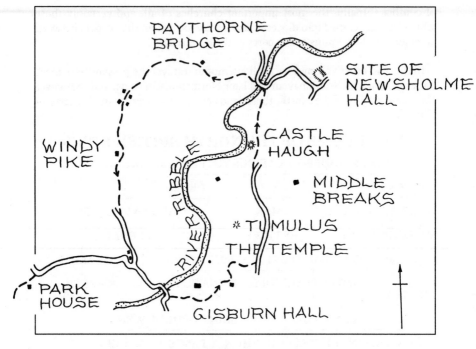

Walk No.1

ABOVE WHERE SALMON LEAP

5 miles, 3 hours.
MAP: *O.S. sheets SD 84/94 & 85/95*
                    PATHFINDER SERIES.
LUNCH: *Gisburn, all the pubs offer good value.*
START: *Gisburn.*

Here where the Ribble turns westwards into Lancashire stand one of the most remarkable monuments in Craven, a huge moated earthwork standing as a sentinel above the river at the portal to the Ribble Valley proper. This and the congenial hidden farmsteads around Gisburn, not forgetting the village itself, make for a ramble of true exploration — a reconnoitre along the edges of the ancient Celtic Cantrev of Craven.

Gisburn to Gisburn Park

After parking your car in the village, take the Bolton-by-Bowland road down to Gisburn Bridge. The Public Right of Way to Gisburn Park is up the lane on the right behind the Gothic Lodge House. Follow the lane up and along the roadway around the lawns of Gisburn Hall.

Gisburn Park

Now a private hospital, Gisburn Park was once the home of the Lister Family, Lords of Ribblesdale. The Listers first came to Craven during the reign of Henry IV, when one John Lyster married Isobel de Bolton and established an estate based at Arnolds Biggin, a farmstead to the south-west of Gisburn village. For three hundred years this was the Hall of the Listers. The Lower Hall, at Gisburn Park, was built in the latter half of the 18th century in a plain Georgian style.

It was some time after this that Thomas Lister was created Baron Ribblesdale for his service in raising a troop to fight in the Napoleonic War with France, and it was he who laid out the Park as we see it today. The many oaks and the double avenue of limes that front the Hall are truly magnificent.

The Listers also kept a large herd of British wild white cattle — the Craven Heifer, remembered by many inn signs throughout the North of England.

The approach to the Park from the south is marked by two fanciful Gothic gate lodges of c.1800. The railway tunnel entrances — Lord Ribblesdale forbade a cutting through his parklands — have heavy castellated parapets befitting the squirely domain. The Gothic lodge by Gisburn Bridge bears eight arms in block brought from Sawley Abbey upon its south wall, and across the way stands the old saw mill with its castellated turrets, a 'fort' William Brown would have been proud to occupy.

Gisburn Park to Castle Haugh

Follow the roadway around the lawns of Gisburn Hall to go through a gate by roadgate. Cross the road to go down a trackway, over Stock Beck Bridge, and on up to follow the track to the main roadway (the Bronze Age Barrow is atop the hill on your left, amid the trees, as you come down to the road). Turn left and walk up the road, past the HORTON/NEWSHOLME boundary stone, to go over stile by gate on left at 'RIBBLE WAY' signs. Turn right and walk up to the right of Castle Haugh to go through gate.

Castle Haugh

On the approach to the Castle we pass a Ditched Bowl Barrow of Bronze Age origin. The tumulus, upon excavation at the turn of the century, yielded several collared urns of the Pennine type, pointing to an early settlement of the region, probably centred on Bolton-by-Bowland, where a number of Bronze Age axe heads and other objects from that period have been found.

These isolated finds provide a tantalising insight into Bronze Age society. However, the evidence we have tends to pose as many questions as they resolve. A ditched bowl barrow is evidence of a society with a level of social organisation capable of converting surplus economic value into funeral monuments. This society supported a primitive ceramic and metallurgy technology and must have conducted trade with peoples outside of Craven, and it was probably a hierarchical warrior society.

The religious beliefs of these folk required the burning of the corpse and the collecting of the unburnt remains in funeral urns. Barrows and cairns containing Pennine type urns have been found throughout the north of England. Not only are these urns widespread in geographical terms — but the practice of crematory urns persisted for over a thousand years well into the Romano-British Iron Age.

These crematory urns are sometimes found in isolation, but more often in groups. Research has shown that the contents of a single urn are often made up of the human remains of more than one person. Certain historians of a morbid persuasion have suggested that this is evidence of slave sacrifice on the death of an aristocrat — a common ancient practice. This explanation is possible but other theories have equal merit.

The Bronze Age people would have lived in family and clan units, bodies were burnt to release the souls of the dead into the air — the realm of the gods. The unburnt remains could have been collected and stored in the urns for the purpose of ancestor worship — the bone relics being the link in the present time with the members of the clan who had passed on.

Their slash and burn farming methods required the clan to move on after a few seasons in a district. Maybe at this stage the urns were placed in the barrow or cairn (possibly the family living hut, now discarded), therefore confirming the social relationship between man, his environment and his gods.

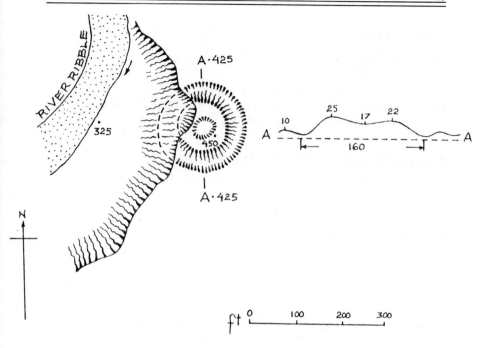

Castle Haugh is sited on the edge of a high scar one hundred feet above the River Ribble south of Paythorne Bridge. It comprises a large mound and surrounding ditch. The central motte is small, twenty-five feet high, and it is evidently defensive, as it still retains the earthen breast work round the top, silted down so as to convert the inner area into a shallow cup. The dry ditch round it, seven feet deep, is nearly perfect, except for a portion that has slipped down the scar. The situation is a commanding one, high above the Ribble, where Ribblesdale meets Craven and Blackburnshire.

Some historians have suggested that Castle Haugh earthwork is what remains of an early castle of the Norman Baron, Roger the Poitevin, mentioned in the Domesday entry for Barnoldswick:

"In Bernulfeswic (including Ellenthorpe), Gamel (the English predecessor of Berenger de Todeni) had 12 carucates for geld. Berenger de Todeni held it, but now it is in the castellate of Roger the Poitevin."

This may be a reference to Castle Haugh, or to Clitheroe Castle, or to some other now lost castle in the West Craven District.

Others suggest that the reference to a 'castellate' is not one to an actual structure but a term used to indicate that a manor was in the honor of a lord. Many other words were used vaguely in the 10th and 11th centuries, before the establishment of an accepted terminology. The word 'castelli' is proven to have been used to refer to the whole of a lord's estates, before the word 'honor' became the norm. This could well be the case with the Barnoldswick Domesday reference. However, the debate goes on.

Castle Haugh to Paythorne Bridge

Pass through the other gate and follow right-hand fence down (Ribble Way) and up to go through gate. Follow track down to Paythorne Bridge.

Paythorne Bridge

Paythorne Bridge links together the ancient Domesday manors of Newsholme and Paythorne, and still retains the mediaeval ribwork under its arches. Of the two old settlements little of an ancient nature remains in view today, except the moated site of Newsholme Hall, with further earthworks to the north-west.

Once a year, on the third Sunday in November, the Bridge is host to a local festival known as 'Salmon Sunday'. The sight of the salmon surmounting the Ribble's many obstacles, each fighting for precedence in the spawning places in the upriver gravelly shallows is one of Nature's joys indeed.

To the east of Paythorne Bridge stands the farmstead of Newsholme Hall. Here considerable earthworks point to a former camera (grange farm) of the wealthy Hospital of St. Leonard, York.

If a light refresher is in order, the Palmers Arms/Buck Inn is only a minutes' walk up the road in Paythorne village.

Paythorne Bridge to Windy Pike

Cross the bridge and go through gate opposite. Follow the track up, through gate, and on to follow wider trackway on, through gate taking right-hand trackway, past the barn and on to where the track veers to the right. Step into the field on the left and walk on to go over fence-stile. Walk on, veering right, down to go over stream and through gateway. Follow left-hand hedgerow up to enter Moor House farmyard. Pass through the farmyard and take the left fork to Windy Pike Farm.

Windy Pike

Windy Pike, with its central jetted porch, is a typical yeoman farmhouse of the late 17th century. And what a splendid view the farmstead boasts, overlooking Craven with the Skipton Aire Gap in the distance and Gisburn Park before it.

At the road junction below Windy Pike at Ellenthorpe Farm, are the kennels of the Gisburn Forest Fox Hounds; you'll be greeted by their yelping and barking when you pass by.

Ellenthorpe was a Domesday settlement linked with Barnoldswick. The link between these settlements was based on agricultural economics. The basic economic unit in mediaeval northern England was the manor. Later in this series this theme will be explored in greater detail, but at this stage the authors would only ask the reader to note the following. Manors in the main valleys of the Pennines tend to encompass the same basic mix of land types; these are upland summer pasture, middle or town lands and low lying riverside winter pasture. Ellenthorpe provided Barnoldswick manor with its summer pastures. With this mixture of land a manor could exist as an independent economic unit. Manors of this type were grouped together to form the basic Celtic unit of land organisation — the multiple estate — which in turn formed together the Celtic Cantrev of Craven.

Windy Pike to Park House/Gisburn

Continue down the farm lane to the roadway. Walk down the road to the junction. The road to the right leads to Park House, and that to the left leads down to Gisburn Bridge and on in to Gisburn.

Park House

Above Fooden, between the Deer Parks of Bolton Hall and Gisburn, stands the Tudor farmstead of Park House. The house is of c.1590 with a two-storeyed gabled porch. Above the round-arched doorway is a stepped four-light window. Within the roof section of the house are the remains of arched braces and kingposts. All going to make a very fine picture to the eye — a true hidden gem.

In the area to the north of Park House a number of Bronze Age artifacts have been turned up by local farmers over the years, the most notable being a half-flanged bronze axehead, that has been placed in the Early Middle Bronze Age period. The axehead, now on display in the Craven Museum at Skipton, is another pointer to the early stable settlement of the region, being at the centre of two important trade routes: the east-west trans-Pennine route and the north-south Ribblesdale/Colne route.

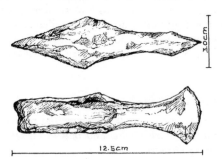

AXEHEAD
HAFT-FLANGED
BRONZE
EARLY M.B.A.
PAYTHORNE
CRAVEN MUSEUM

ST MARY
GISBURN

St. Mary's Church, Gisburn

The Parish Church of St. Mary displays a short Norman tower with a very plain original tower arch. The doorway with continuous mouldings is 13th century. The nave and chancel are for the most part Perpendicular, but the three stepped lancet lights on the west aisle windows look to be c.1290, as do the chancel arch and the west arches of the chancel chapels. Some fragments of 15th century stained glass displaying figures are to be found in one south and one north window. The two Chalices with Communion Plates are dated 1618 and 1696.

An early dedication of the church was to St. Mary the Virgin and St. Andrew given by the Patrons of the Living, the Prioress and the nuns of Stainfield Nunnery in Lincolnshire of that name, in the 13th century. The Nuns shared joint patronage with the Archbishop of York. First mention of a church at Gisburn is for 1140 when one Renulf was priest. Some time later we hear of the rector of Gisburn Church being present at the foundation of Sawley Abbey in 1147. The Stainfield convent was founded by the Percy family. The Convent Grange farm was at Rayhead in Gisburn Forest, hence their connection with St. Mary's. At the north-east end of the churchyard is a house known as the 'Priory'. It is reputed that a former building on the site was used by the Nuns from Rayhead.

Gisburn Church also claims a Catholic Martyr: Richard Simpson, the local minister and schoolmaster, rejected Protestantism and became a Catholic. For this he was arrested and imprisoned at York. Upon release he became a Roman Catholic priest and was hounded throughout Lancashire and Yorkshire. He was finally captured in 1588, tried and condemned to death. In July 1588 he was executed near Derby with two others, 'their heads and quarters set upon poles in divers places'.

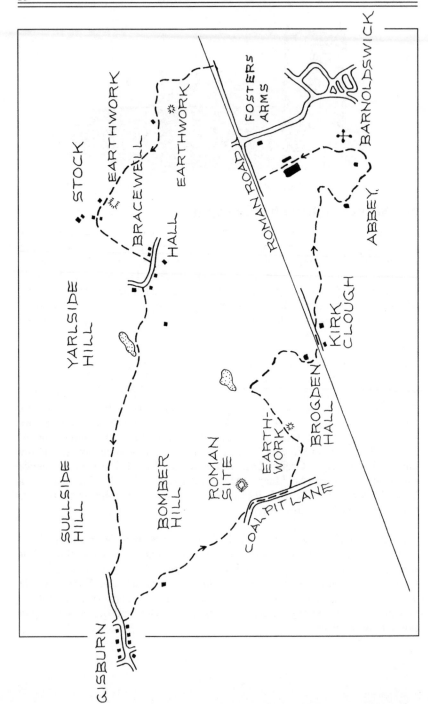

Walk No.2

KING'S REFUGE WITHIN A TEMPEST

10 miles, 5 hours.

Map:	*O.S. Sheet SD 84/94 PATHFINDER SERIES.*
LUNCH:	*Fosters Arms, Barnoldswick or any inn in Gisburn.*
START:	*Gisburn or Barnoldswick.*

We have surveyed the rolling landscape of West Craven from the heights of Newsholme on the previous walk; now let us be off among the morain floor below the Pendle Grits to discover an 'El Dorado' of historic sites. Whether started from Gisburn or the Fosters Arms in Barnoldswick nothing detracts from the pleasure to be gained from this easygoing and most enjoyable walk.

Gisburn Village

Once the home of Sir Guy of Gisburn the tormentor of Robin Hood, the village remains today a simple market centre serving the outlying parish farmsteads. The charter for Gisburn Fair was granted by Henry III to the convent of Sawley Abbey in 1260, the market to be held every Monday, and a fair every year of three days' duration on the Eve, Day and Morrow of the birth of the Blessed Virgin Mary (8th September).

In those times it was held in the main street, and a photograph taken before the war shows the cattle market held outside the Ribblesdale Arms. Today the cattle market is to be found on the west approach to the village, and the traditional market has given way to Sunday car-boot sales, the haunt of modern day rogues and vagabonds — a disgrace and an insult to the Sabbath.

Our research has shown that the most popular date for fairs in Yorkshire was the feast of the Blessed Virgin (September 8th). Under the old calendar the feast fell in late August after harvest. These fairs allowed the peasant to dispose of surplus cattle and produce before the winter. These fairs to towns or lords of the manors who held a charter as tolls could be charged on goods and stock sold. Gisburn was the main fair for middle Ribblesdale and the upper Aire. Lower down the Ribble fairs and markets existed at Whalley and Clitheroe, and to the east of Gisburn at Skipton, Otley, Knaresborough and Pateley.

One might wonder why a fair which served an area of about 10 to 15 miles radius could last for three days? Surely considering the level of economic activity most surplus goods could be exchanged in a few hours of the first day. But the pace of commerce was much slower then, and the trade was only one aspect of the fair. Court Rolls reveal that fairs were occasions of social intercourse, renewing friendships, settling debts and old scores.

Ready cash attracted the ale sellers, disputes concerning trade transactions, tolls and local rivalry fuelled by drink could lead to serious disorder. Later in the series we will see that the the dispute between the men of Knaresborough Forest and the Archbishops fairs at Pateley and Otley continued for many generations and could degenerate into manslaughter.

The majority of buildings in the village date from the rebuilding of the 1850's by the Ribblesdale Estate, a Victorian monotony broken tastefully by an array of late 17th century buildings. The proudest of these stands opposite the church gates, being a three-storeyed pile with a great deal of ancient original internal timberwork. On the western approach to the village, sandwiched between two buildings, is an old farmhouse with mullioned windows, the doorhead bearing a date of 1705.

On a back lane, across from the Ribblesdale Arms are two cottages, one bearing a date of 1674 and the other displaying the date 1675 with the initials RA.AA.TA. The lane itself is a pleasing backwater away from the busy main street — if any village deserved a by-pass from the intrusions of road transport it has to be Gisburn, cut in half by a swathe of fume-belching vehicles.

By far the grandest frontage is that belonging to the Ribblesdale Arms, 17th century above blending down to 19th century re-modelling. Above the porch doorway a tablet informs one that the inn was originally built in 1635, and that Thomas Lister (of Gisburn Park) rebuilt the front at his own cost in 1855.

On August 16th 1648, General Oliver Cromwell and General Lambert, on their way to meet with the Royalist force at Preston, halted at Gisburn with Sir John Assheton of Downham, leader of the Lancashire Militia, to hold a council of war. It is said that the stained glass windows in the church were smashed at this time.

However, research conducted by Robert Whiting has shown that many local traditions blaming the breaking of windows and images by Parliamentary forces during the Civil Wars are incorrect. Most of the damage to mediaeval church heritage was carried out by local protestants in the 16th century Reformation.

The slur on the name of Oliver Cromwell is difficult to understand — Parliamentary forces did carry out certain atrocities in Scotland and Ireland. Royalist forces are clearly documented to have committed atrocities in the Midlands, south-west and north-west of England. On the whole the Parliamentary army and the later New Model Army had a reputation for iron discipline and was not noted for petty vandalism.

It may be difficult to accept today when the monarchy is a bastion of legal authority, tradition and order, that the monarchy once unleashed for partly selfish motives a programme of iconoclasm. The windows and images that once graced the churches of Craven were probably broken sixty years before Cromwell was born.

Being so near to the hill of Pendle the village is not without its tales of witchcraft. In 1612, Jennet Preston of Gisburn-in-Craven was arrested and charged with the murder of Thomas Lister of Westby Hall (Arnold's Biggin). Five years previously Jennet had been tried at York in connection with the death of a child at Westby but the judge found no fault with her. On this second occasion at York before Judge Altham, evidence was presented against her by Robert 'Witchfinder' Nowell of Read Hall, and the Magistrate Thomas Herber of Marton, whose daughter was married to the reigning Thomas Lister.

It was stated that she plotted with the witches of Malkin Tower in Pendle to bring about the death of Thomas Lister by means of charms and sorcery, given his former persecution of her over the death of the child. The witnesses swore on oath that Thomas on his death bed cried out unto them that stood about him that Jennet Preston was in the house. "Look where she is, take hold of her, for God's sake shut the doors and take her so she cannot escape away".

Upon Lister's death Jennet was brought to the house and bidden to touch the body, whereupon it bled fresh blood. The bleeding of a corpse, they held, could only come about by the touch of the murderer. On such spurious evidence Jennet was found guilty and hanged, 'impenitent and void of all fear and grace'.

Gisburn to Bomber Camp

As you come out of the churchyard walk up to the Settle turning on the roadway and cross the road to go under the archway opposite. Walk up the lane to go over wall-stile at junction. Walk up the field on a left diagonal to short section of walling and wall-stile (DO NOT GO OVER WALL-STILE). From the wall-stile walk on a right diagonal to go over fence at corner. Follow left-hand hedgerow to enter Moor Laithe farmyard. Follow the farm lane to the left, through gate and on to go through next gate. Walk up the hill and down to far left-hand corner to go through gate. Cross the field veering slightly to the left, over the hill and down to go over fence-stile on left. Cross the field on a right diagonal to enter Coal Pit Lane by fence-stile in hedgerow forty yards before the corner. Left, and walk along the lane to gateway on the left. Bomber Camp is over in the next field in front of you.

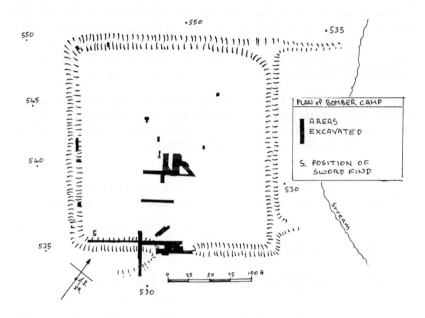

Bomber Camp

Bomber Camp, named after the nearby Bomber Farm, is a large square earthwork with surrounding ditch that owes its origins to the Roman period. The site was excavated in 1940 by the archaeologist, R. C. Musson. The camp lies on the south slope of a small hill and is approximately square, with sides roughly 200 x 220 feet, being one acre inside the shallow ditch which encloses it. The entry to the enclosure was seen to be in the centre of the south-east side, the position of post-holes being noted. The limited dig inside the camp revealed both cobbled and paved surfaces and a number of post-holes.

Finds from the camp included an iron sword, an upper quern stone, remains of three mortaria (Crambeck Type 6, common in the 4th century), and fragments of 4th century Samian copies, a stone spindle whorle, a stone pounder and numerous other fragments of fine buff and thin grey ware. No hearths were found, though some of the pottery showed signs of burning.

During the 1970's the site was again subjected to excavation, this time by a group of local amateur archaeologists (their site cabin still stands on the site at the time of writing, September 1989). Unfortunately the group disbanded without any reports being made. However, sources inform the author that a number of circular quern stones and an amount of Samian(?) and other pottery were found and are now in private hands. Also, recent aerial photography has identified other earthworks near to the north-west of the site that appear to be contemporary with the camp.

So what does Bomber Camp represent? We would argue for a 4th century Romano-British farmstead, built within a semi-defensive, regular enclosure, which had been paved in a rough manner. We think that a full plan of the post-holes would point to a native copy of a Roman villa.

This villa/homestead, of some local chief, was burnt/abandoned in c.365 during civil unrest. The sword, quern stones and the broken and burnt pots in the enclosure itself, do tend to point to a violent termination of settlement.

The camp stands one mile north of the Roman Road between the forts of Ribchester and Elslack.

Bomber Camp to Primrose Hill Earthwork

Walk on along Coal Pit Lane to go through gate on the left. Walk up the field on a right diagonal and on down to go over fence-stile and stream. Walk up the hill to go over fence-stile by gate. Pass through the gate and follow right-hand hedgerow to opening in fence. Walk through the opening onto the Earthwork.

Primrose Hill Earthwork

This earthwork, thought to mark the site of a Roman signal tower, is situated 500m. north of the Ribchester to Elslack Roman Road, it measures 10m. square, the top of the platform being 1m. above the surrounding field level.

During June 1971 the site was excavated by Alan King and the Chorley College of Education. No post-holes or masonry were found, nor any finds. There was no ditch around the earthwork, but the boulder clay of the mound contained sandstone while the drift below was more calcareous, and so it was given to be man-made.

The site is well positioned to view the country to the north and east, especially towards the earthwork known as Bomber Camp. Again, as before, I consider that a further investigation is more than needed.

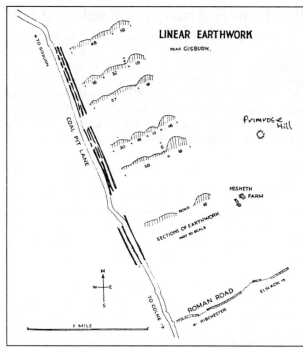

Coal Pit Lane

Coal Pit Lane, otherwise known as Gisburn Old Road, forms for the major part of its length the boundary between the Ribble Valley and Pendle Districts.

The name refers to marginal coal quarrying on the lower flanks of Weets Hill.

During his time at Gisburn, Musson surveyed a two-mile section of the lane and put forward the proposal that it formed part of a Linear Earthwork. The form of the earthwork is ridge and ditch (see plan) — three parallel lines of raised banks with a ditch in between them.

He wondered whether there was any connection between the Roman road, the Romano/British camp and the intervening earthwork on Primrose Hill. He concluded that the earthwork was man made as a barrier or boundary, and that it was probably constructed before the Norman Conquest.

I have examined the earthworks several times and must report that little evidence as to their existence remains today. This is due to the ridges having been removed to mix with lime for spreading on the fields over the last fifty years or more.

Coal Pit Lane is today a wide, deeply rutted track, a deep hollow-way in places. Could not the ridges have been a part of this once much used highway? Even so one cannot dismiss their possible connection with Bomber Camp without further evidence.

Primrose Hill to Fosters Arms, via Monkroyd Hill

Walk back through the opening and follow right-hand hedgerow to go over wide stile on right of gate overlooking the reservoir. Follow right-hand fence/hedgerow, then stream to go over footbridge. Walk on to go through gate in wall on the right. Follow left-hand hedgerow up, through gateposts, following fence/wall into Brogden Hall farmyard. Walk through the farmyard to go left down Brogden Lane, then right at the 'Barnoldswick' footpath-sign at Kirk Clough. Follow lane up to go through gate. Follow left-hand wall then hedgerow to go through small gate by gate onto farm track.

Walk along the track opposite to go through small gate by gate into field. Cross the field on a right diagonal to go through stile by gate. Walk up and over the hill on a right diagonal to go through gateway in hedge. Follow old trackway down to go over fence-stile. Cross stream and follow left-hand hedgerow to stile by gate. Turn right and follow the track up to go over stile. Follow track to the left to go through gate by side of Cow Pasture Farm (dated I.M.E. 1848). Walk down the drive to go through gateway onto lane.

Follow lane on and down, over the cattle-grid, to go through kissing-gate by gate set back on the left (Barnoldswick Abbey was sited somewhere near this spot). Walk up Monkroyd Hill and over and down to go over fence-stile. Cross the field to go through stile onto pathway. Follow the path, through the factory yard and into field via gate. Walk directly on, over the hill and on down to go over stile in hedge. Walk on to go over stile onto Brogden Lane. Turn right and walk down to the main road. Right, and walk on to the Fosters Arms.

Monkroyde

Monkroyde is the name given to an area of land lying to the north of the village of Barnoldswick that was once owned by the monks of Kirkstall Abbey. 'The Monk's Clearing' is thought by many to be the site of the ancient Barnoldswick Abbey. The Cistercian abbey of the Blessed Virgin Mary was founded at Barnoldswick in 1147 by Henry de Lacy, Baron of Pontefract, a daughter house of Fountains Abbey.

And so it was, in this reign of Stephen when anarchy raged throughout the land, that on the 19th May, 1147, Alexander, the Prior, twelve monks and ten lay brothers set forth from Fountains for the remote land of Barnoldswick. Once here they erected wooden living quarters, a chapel and mill for the service of God under their 'Charter of Charity'. By 1152 the monks had abandoned their Craven site and moved to the site of a hermitage at Kirkstall.

In the words of one of the monks "the place of our dwelling was at first called Bernulfeswick, which we having changed name, call St. Mary's Mount. We stayed there for some years, suffering many discomforts of hunger and cold, partly by reason of the inclemency of the air, and immoderate plague of waters, partly because of the Kingdom being disturbed, robbers many times wasted our goods".

There are many instances where monastic communities brought about the destruction or movement of settlements and churches. There is some evidence that this may have happened at and around Barnoldswick. As to the site of the Barnoldswick monastic buildings, these must have been located at the centre of the now modern township. Others place the site near to St. Mary's Well, just below Monkroyde hill.

Fosters Arms

The Fosters Arms stands by the side of Gisburn Road on the edge of the village. Formerly named Syke House, the inn bears two datestones: above the doorway, C.H. 1699 R.B., and by the far right window, C.H. 1688 (possibly Heber of Marton). The Fosters Arms provides a good lunch stop, good beer and food being always available.

Fosters Arms to Stock

From the inn walk down to go left down Gisburn Road, then right to go down Greenber Field Lane to Broad Ing Bridge. Once over the bridge pass over the wall-stile on the left. Cross the field directly to go over stile, and on across the next field to go over footbridge on the left. Walk on around the base of Gilbeber Hill to ruined field barn.

Go over stile in wall to the left of the barn. Walk on up the hill to turn right just before the summit to make your way down to go over footbridge at corner of far hedgerow. Follow the hedgerow over the flank of Hawber Hill to go over wall-stile over on the left. Walk down to the farm road between Stock Cottage and barn.

Stock Hamlet

The hamlet of Stock is situated in a hollow formed by three small hills (drumlins), and is divided from the hamlet of Bracewell by Stock Beck, which is the main watercourse in the area.

The hamlet is first mentioned in the Norman Survey of 1086 — "In Stoche, Archil had 4 carucates for geld" (the carucate was in theory the area which a single eight-ox plough-team could plough in a single year; the bovate was usually an eighth of this. It has been suggested that in Yorkshire bovates were normally 8 and 15 acres in extent, but that they could contain as few as 4 acres and as many as 28. Most references to carucates are probably to fiscal areas rather than to genuine agricultural units).

The place-name 'stock' can mean two things: a stockade, or a secondary settlement. It is significant that the main watercourse in the area is named after the settlement and not Bracewell or Barnoldswick.

Though today Stock comprises only three dwelling houses and a small number of related farm buildings, the surrounding earthworks — platforms, banks, ridges and hollows — point to a much larger settlement at one time. There is no historical record of this 'larger' settlement, only the surviving farms, and therefore we must date it as prior to the 14th century (the County Archaeological Record classes the site as a Deserted Mediaeval Village — DMV).

It may be that Stock is a secondary settlement to Bracewell — an ancient hollow-way leads from Stock to Bracewell Church, but without a full archaeological investigation the question must remain unsettled.

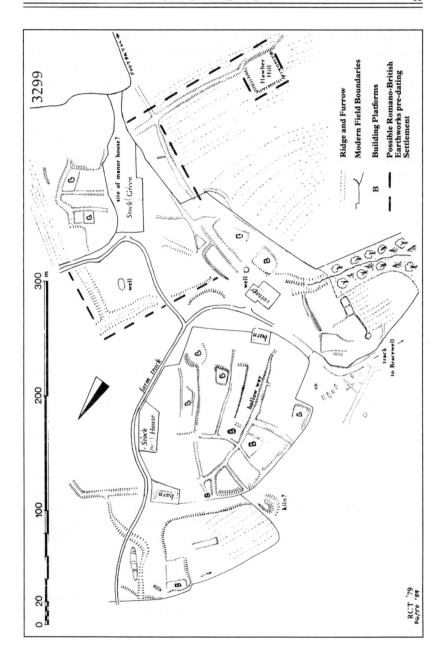

3299

Ridge and Furrow

Modern Field Boundaries

B   Building Platforms

Possible Romano-British
Earthworks pre-dating
Settlement

RCT '79
DG/TD '89

The evidence of the Norman Survey and field archaeology point to an Anglo-Saxon origin for this settlement. A community of no more than 10 to 15 households — or fewer than sixty souls. This means that the population of mediaeval Craven was probably less than 1/20th of the present population of the modern local government area.

The number of persons living directly off the land was clearly higher than that today. The present day parish of Bracewell is made up of two Domesday manors, this area supports only a fraction of the Domesday level of population in farming pursuits.

Near to the settlement of Stock are two hill-top earthworks; one is sited above Stock upon Hawber Hill, the other is sited upon Gilbeber Hill, roughly 30 yards square and 27 yards square respectively.

The Hawber earthwork has a hollow-way running up to it from Stock Green, the line of which continues from the earthwork down to Stock Beck in the form of a raised mound. The Gilbeber earthwork displays signs of an outer ditch, and both sites command a view of the surrounding area that is bisected by the Roman road.

There are over a dozen such hill enclosure sites in the western central Pennine area and none, other than the Bomber Camp/Primrose Hill sites, have been subject to archaeological study. At this stage it may be reasonable to view the Hawber and Gilbeber site as having their possible origins in the late Roman period. And, in the case of Hawber, may be related to some of the earthwork features around Stock Green that we consider may be a Romano-British settlement site similar to that of Bomber Camp.

Whitaker, in his "History of Craven", states that "tradition holds that they (the Hawber and Gilbeber earthworks) were constructed by the Royalist forces of Prince Rupert during their march through Craven in 1644. They consist of small square encampments and are strengthened by long rectilinear fosses, which descend along the slope of the hills on each side to the plane beneath."

Tradition also held that Bomber Camp was a Civil War fortification or a paddock for the Galloway ponies which acted as pack horses over the hills in the last century. No such construction works for this part of Craven during the Civil Wars are recorded, as then, one can only speculate as to their true nature.

Stock to Bracewell

Follow the wall at the front of the barn to go through gate. Follow the hollow-way up and round to the left and on down to go over footbridge. Follow path on, over stile, following left-hand hedgerow up to go through gateway to Bracewell Church.

ST. MICHAEL
BRACEWELL
SOUTH DOOR

Bracewell Church

On raised ground above the road-way stands the small attractive church of St Michael, once the private chapel of the Tempest family.

Richard Tempest was granted the Manor of Bracewell in 1085 and a short time after built his chapel in the Norman style, of which several features remain today: the south doorway displays one order of columns with scalloped capitals supporting a single-step arch; the chancel arch set on scalloped corbels; and the lower section of the 15th century tower. The font is 12th century, simple without ornamentation. The west window of the aisle, having reticulated tracery could be of c.1350.

Also in the aisle are two niches known as the Tempest niches dating from c.1500, being unusual as they are set in the piers of the north arcade. In Craven this only occurs in the Tempest churches, being at Bracewell, Broughton and Kirkby Malham. To the south-west of the tower stands an archway, being all that remains of the manor house that was demolished in 1656, rebuilt on its present site.

King Henry's Parlour

To the south-west of the church stands the pre-Reformation house (now a barn-type building) known as Henry VI's Parlour. It is said that Henry, whilst fleeing from his foes after the Battle of Hexham (1464), hid here before taking refuge with the Pudseys of Bolton Hall, Bolton-by-Bowland.

The building is much restored but a straight-headed window with ogee-arched top is recognisable, but this appears to be a composite of various fragments of masonry (the window head appears to have a date carved upon it 1625, I think). This is borne out when we look at the upper side window of the building, here we have what the former window would originally have looked like: perpendicular, straight-headed of two ogee-headed tri-foil light, with carved heads on the drip-mould lugs.

In the fields behind the church and Parlour are a number of earthworks. These are related to the old Bracewell Hall of the Tempest family and other associated buildings.

Bracewell to Gisburn

Walk up the Gisburn road to go left at the bend along the farm lane, right at the fork, on, over cattle-grid and down passing the lake to go over next cattle-grid, then go over fence-stile on the right. Walk down to go over footbridge, then walk up to the left to enter wood by wall-stile. Follow path up through the wood to go over fence-stile onto hillside. On a left diagonal walk over the hill to the left of the five-barred gate and on down to go over the wall-stile. Walk up the field on a left diagonal to go over wall-stile (good views over Pendle and the surrounding countryside are to be had from here). On a right diagonal walk down the hill to go through small fence-gate, and continue on the same line to go over fence-stile and on across the field to go over next fence-stile. Walk on up and over the brow of the hill to go over fence-stile. Follow old hedgerow on the right to go over stile and on over next stile. Follow the mound of the old trackway down and across the field to go over stile onto roadway at farm lane entrance. Left, and follow the road on into Gisburn.

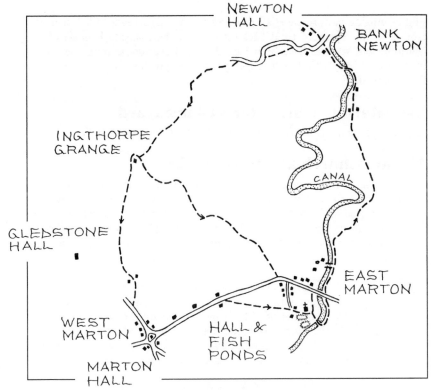

Walk No.3

MANORS WEST OF THE TOW-PATH

5½ or 4½ miles, 4 or 3 hours.
MAP: *O.S. sheet 85/95*
                PATHFINDER SERIES
LUNCH: *Cross Keys Inn, East Marton*
START: *East Marton*

For many who walk the 'Pennine Way', the Martons both and Bank Newton are passed by in the push to Gargrave — a common failing of most long distance paths. Yet other's folly in not tarrying awhile is our gain. Amid rolling hillside pasture we shall discover yeoman farmsteads still lost to the crowds in this splendid rural backwater. Even the roadside hamlets of the Martons both seem to have been passed by and overlooked by modern contrivances, a remarkable but true fact given their position on the busy trans-Pennine road.

East Marton to St. Peter's Churchyard

A path opposite the Cross Keys Inn leads directly to the churchyard.

Marton Church and Earthworks

The Church of St. Peter at Marton was founded in the 12th century and came under the authority of Kirkstall Abbey (re. Barnoldswick Abbey), but by 1186 it was being administered by the Canons of Bolton who, as patrons, were responsible for the appointment of Rectors. Bolton paid 20s. each year to the Abbey at Kirkstall as an acknowledgement of the church's original dependence upon the Abbey.

The building comprises a short Norman tower and a 19th century chancel and nave, the latter containing some small bits of Norman decoration in the north wall. A dated sundial of 1714 is mounted upon the south wall of the tower. Once inside the church we notice the roughly hewn Norman font standing upon an old grindstone supported by three rounded stones. Close inspection of the font reveals some evidence of decoration, though barely visible.

Standing by the font is a fragment of a Late Anglo-Saxon cross of Viking style, carved from Knaresborough stone. This very fine piece depicts the Norse god Thor with his hammer, enmeshed in conflict with the Earth Serpent, coiled around all four faces of the shaft. The cross was found near St.

Helen's Hill upon the River Wharfe, two miles below Thorp Arch. It was brought here from Scriven Park, a gift to the church from a member of the Roundell family.

Also inside the church are memorials to the Heber and Roundell families, the former having three Rectors of Marton within their number in the years between 1679 and 1799, and one, Reginald Heber, who was Bishop of Calcutta (1823-1826).

The Martons were the first lords of the manor of Marton, and it was they who first erected a Hall upon the rise to the south of the churchyard. The site of their Hall of c.1445 is marked today by a series of clearly defined earthworks, the lower of which are the ancient fish ponds of Marton Hall. In these ponds were kept a variety of fish, including eels as well as crayfish. Fish ponds are one of the features of mediaeval life, arising largely from the difficulty of obtaining fresh meat in winter.

East Marton Churchyard to Bank Newton

Pass through the small gate on the south-east of the churchyard and walk on to the canal tow-path. Walk along the tow-path, under the double arched bridge, to leave via 'Pennine Way' at next bridge. Follow lane to the right and on to go through stile on the right at 'Pennine Way' sign. Follow path to the left, around the wood and over stiles to cross field into lane. Follow lane to the right to Newton Grange Farm and on, over the canal, down to Bank Newton. Newton Hall stands opposite the crossroads.

Bank Newton

The charming Locks and associated canal cottages represent only half of the attractions at Bank Newton. The other is to be found in the 17th century dwellings of Bank Newton Farm and Newton Hall. The former is a period cottage set within a walled garden that in the summer months is a wild profusion of colour, a credit to its owners and a joy for the eye to behold.

Across the way stands the proud edifice of Newton Hall, with its impressive gable end of four rows of mullioned windows. Immediately adjoining the Hall on the north-east is a little chantry, now an out-house in the garden, near to which many bones are said to have been dug up.

On this building Whitaker, in his 'History of Craven', says: "From the shape of one of the original windows yet remaining, I should conjecture this

humble foundation to be as old as the Cattertons (c.1300). In an adjoining out-house, but probably removed from this chapel, is a large inscription in the character of Henry VIII's time — IHS HELPE."

Bank or Cald Newton Hall was the seat of the Banks family for three centuries, sold by the last of their line to Nicholas Towneley of Royle in Lancashire. Later it was the home of the Coulthurst family, noted landowners in Craven. The aisled barn at the rear of the Hall is also worthy of note.

Chantry chapels were a major feature of popular piety in the later Middle Ages. The chantry was normally a private endowment in real property to ensure masses for the souls of the founder and his kin. The incumbent who drew the stipend usually said these masses at a particular altar in a church, or here at Newton Hall — a chapel built next to the manor house of the patrons.

Chantry chapels were suppressed by an Act of the Edwardian Reformation Parliament in 1548. Camden records that at this time 2374 chantries, 90 colleges and 110 hospitals were supressed. Since the Pilgrimage of Grace rebellion in 1536 the chantry at Newton Hall had been vacant, and the patrons had reclaimed its endowments. However, this action was to no avail, for the Royal Court insisted that the endowments be surrendered to the commissioners.

It was not uncommon for a tract of land given by a family to a chantry for masses would be sold back to the same family. A chantry endowment in

Yorkshire was usually only £5 to £7 per year which was in 16th century money terms the wage of a labourer. The priest at Newton Hall would have supplemented his meager stipend by doing other work, probably as schoolmaster for the patron's children and as his private secretary.

The funds obtained by this 16th century form of Nationalisation were supposed to help found secular hospitals and schools — but this rarely happened. The funds were used to bolster the finances of the Royal Court.

Besides the thirty or so chantry chapels that existed in mediaeval Craven there was a host of Grange and private chapels. Later in this walk we will encounter a grange chapel at Ingthorpe. A grange was an 'outfarm' of a monastic estate.

When first established Granges were staffed by monks and lay brothers who required a chapel so that they could follow the daily cycle of prayer. After the plague of 1348 most granges were let out to lay tenants — and the grange chapel either became private chapels or fell into disuse. A private chapel did not have a stipendary priest to say masses on a daily basis — but would be used mainly for the daily prayers of the household.

A fourth type of chapel was a Chapel of Ease of a mother church. In the north of England parishes were so large that the population of outlying districts could not attend services. The chapel of ease was provided for the convenience of the inhabitants of outlying areas. Certain chapels of ease were later raised to the status of a parish church it their own right.

The Settlement of 1689 and the Catholic Act of Toleration led to the establishment of many new chapels — not to be confused with the chapels of the mediaeval church. The study of mediaeval and later chapels in Craven is an area which would reward further research by local historians.

On our way to Bank Newton, before the locks, we passed through Newton Grange Farm, a name recalling the many ancient monastic farmsteads in the Craven area.

Newton Hall to Ingthorpe Grange

Left, and walk down the road passing barn and house to go through field-gate on the left. Follow stream up to where it bends to the right and walk on across the field, veering left, to go over wall-stile onto road. Follow road on, to the left, to go over wall-stile on left opposite hawthorn bush. On a right diagonal, cross the stream and on over the base of the hill to climb the next hill to go through small gate in wall. On a left diagonal walk over the brow of the hill to go through gate in fence down over on the right. Walk directly up the hill, then drop down to the right to go through field-gate. Walk up the rise, veering to the left, over and on down to go over fence-stile, stream and wall-stile. Pass through the gate over on the right to cross the field on a left diagonal to enter Ingthorpe Grange farmyard by green gate.

Ingthorpe Grange

Ingthorpe is first mentioned in the Norman Survey of 1086, then called Ucnetorp (Unnkell's outlying farmstead), where Uctred and Archil had two carucates for geld. Tradition holds that the early hamlet was destroyed by the Scots in the early 14th century, remains of which are said to have been clearly visible in the early 1800's (more probably of the later monastic grange).

ING THORPE GRANGE

In c.1300 a bercary (sheep farm) was established here by the monks of Bolton Priory; before that, c.1295, it was farmed out for wheat. In 1320 four ploughmen are recorded as being employed at Ingthorpe. The Canons of Bolton Priory paid a regular pension to the Abbots and monks of Kirkstall Abbey as representatives of the old monastery at Barnoldswick in consideration of the whole of Marton including Ingthorpe.

The Canons seem to have had a small cell and chapel at Ingthorpe as a basso relievo in white marble from the frieze on the back of an altar was found here in the early 1800's.

The subject of which seems to have the apprehension of Christ with Peter drawing his sword. The whole is 13 inches long and 11 inches wide.

After the Dissolution the Grange was granted to the 1st Earl of Cumberland in 1542, whose grandson sold the estate to the Baldwins, builders of the present house.

The house presents a gabled frontage of mullioned windows with a porch of three storeys and two round-headed doorways. Above the first floor window of the porch is a triangular panel informing us that ' **** BALDWEN BIRTH WAS 1671', below the window is the datestone of the house, H.B.B. 1672. To the rear of the house can be found a Y-tracery church-style window. Could the house have once had its own chapel?

The walk can now be shortened by a direct return to East Marton by following Ingthorpe Lane, the track at the front of the house, down to the village.

Ingthorpe Grange to Mire House

Walk through the farmyard to the rear of the barn to go through gate (notice the Y-tracery chapel window) and follow left-hand wall, then fence to corner and on to go through far gateway. Follow track on, through gate, to the front of Mire House.

WEST MARTON
MIRE HOUSE

Mire House

Mire House is a substantial 17th century farmhouse hidden away in this rural backwater of Marton, let's hope that such places continue to exist for many ages yet to come contributing to our vernacular architectural heritage.

Mire House to West Marton

Follow lane on to roadway, left, and on in to West Marton.

WEST MARTON

West Marton

West Marton is a tiny roadside hamlet that grew up around the old West Marton Hall and the more recent Gledstone Hall. The latter stands between the village and Ingthorpe, a classical style house built by Sir Edwin Lutyens in 1925-7. This replaced an earlier late 18th century hall of which the kennels and stables still remain. The village shop has a dated doorhead, 1690, and around the corner is a barn dated 1668 with the initials I.I.S. By the crossroads stand the village stocks, and below these can be found the farmstead of Marton Hall which still retains some of its original features. Thomas Marton sold West Marton Hall to Thomas Heber of Elslack c.1535, and around 1600, Lancellot Marton sold East Marton Hall to the Hebers.

West Marton to East Marton Church

Walk along Skipton Road to go through kissing-gate by gateway on right after passing the Old School House. Cross the field on a left diagonal to go through gate in fence by short section of walling. Walk on and down the hill to go through gate onto lane by converted barn. Walk down the lane to the Church.

From the north-east corner of the churchyard a path follows the right-hand wall/fence on over to the Cross Keys Inn at East Marton.

EAST MARTON

East Marton

After refreshing yourself in the delightfully quaint Cross Keys Inn we suggest a stroll around the village down to Abbots Harbour.

Above the inn stands a typical 17th century Dales cottage with a most unusual doorhead, dated 1698 with the initials A.A.A., very picturesque. Down by the canal we find Abbots Harbour, serving traditional farmhouse food in a 17th century setting. The house next door is Sawley House, a former grange of Sawley Abbey. Notice the two small lancet windows on the upper floor, 13th century remains built into a later 17th century house.

East Marton stands above Crickle Beck, an Old Welsh (British) placename referring to an artificial hill or barrow. Crickle Farm is a 17th century building, with a central three-storeyed gabled porch, that is worth viewing.

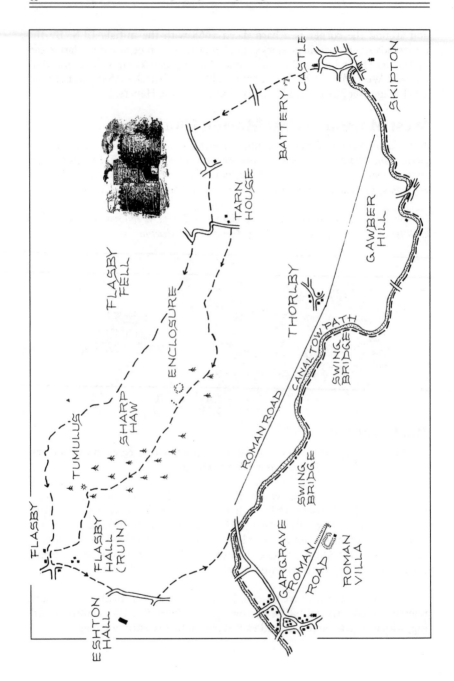

Walk No.4

CRAVEN STRONGHOLDS

11½ miles, 6 to 7 hours.
Map: *O.S. sheet SD 85/95*
                  PATHFINDER SERIES.
LUNCH: *Any inn in Skipton or Gargrave.*
START: *Skipton or Gargrave (but suggest Skipton).*

In this walk we take in the rugged splendour of the highlands above the market town of Skipton. To the north north east rises Rylstone Fell and Embsay Moor, a great wilderness from where the stones were hewn to build the castle and town of Skipton. The quarry roads can still be followed leading to such places as Crookrise, Fairies Chest, Deer Gallows and Stone Ridge quarries. To the north west our route is marked by the pike of Sharp Haw, sentinel to the upper Aire Valley, from which vantage point the lay of Craven is overviewed. We descend quickly from the rough gritstones of Flasby Fell to the locks east of Gargrave to return by way of the towing path to Skipton town.

Skipton Castle

The lands around Skipton were granted to the Norman Baron Robert de Romille between 1086 and 1100 and he may have built the first castle on the site; if so, nothing from that early date remains. His successors did, we know, build a castle in the 12th century, of which only a Norman arch in the passage leading to the courtyard of the castle, the Conduit Court, remains. In 1284 the castle was granted to Robert de Clifford who built virtually a new castle, before he was killed at Bannockburn in 1314. The building was damaged during the Scottish wars and was restored by the third Lord Clifford, who succeeded to the title in 1322, from which time the castle has been added to, and contains work from many different periods.

Entry to the castle is gained by passing through the rotund portal of the Outer Gatehouse, whose twin drum towers stand sentinel at the head of the town. Above the archway are the arms of Clifford, and on the wallhead, in stone letters, the Clifford motto, DESORMAIS (Henceforth).

Once through the gate passage we enter the outer bailey and view the castle proper, a palatial pile dating from the early 14th century, with extensions and rebuilding over the years. The tower before us is the Watch Tower, one of six original circular towers that formed the main structure of the castle. These towers were once much higher, but the slighting of the castle as a result of the Civil War much reduced their size.

The·Castle·Gateway

Skipton Castle was the only Royalist stronghold in the North after the battle of Marston

Moor and put up a prolonged resistance from 1642 until Sir John Mallory surrendered it under honourable terms in December 1645. Some years later the castle was ordered to be made untenable. Only after 1650 did Lady Anne Clifford begin the work of restoration whose results we view today.

There are many other features of Skipton Castle which one could describe here, but these, and a full history of the Castle, are to be found in the Castle Guide Book, on sale at the Gatehouse gift shop.

Holy Trinity Parish Church

A church was first established at Skipton in the early 12th century, but of this nothing remains, the present edifice being for the most part Perpendicular with some Decorated remains.

The Church, with the Chapel of Carleton and the village of Embsay, formed the original endowment of the Priory of Embsay, later Bolton Priory, and was under the care of the Canons of Bolton till 1326, when a vicarage was endowed by Archbishop Melton. At the Dissolution it was given to the Dean and Canons of Christ Church, Oxford, who are the present patrons of the living.

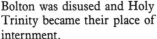

Worthy of note inside the church are the Clifford Tombs and their accompanying brasses. Bolton Priory was the place of burial for the Cliffords, but after the Dissolution the vault at

Bolton was disused and Holy Trinity became their place of internment.

The Cliffords Tombs ~ Skipton Church ~ Yorks.

The tombs number three and are: Henry, 1st Earl of Cumberland, and Margaret Percy, his wife (1542), with good brass effigies, 3ft 6in. long, on the black marble top (the tomb case is Purbeck marble); Francis, son of George, Earl of Cumberland (1589). This tomb was badly damaged during the Civil War seige and the brasses

stolen; George, 3rd Earl of Cumberland, and father of the last named (1605), elaborately ornamented with armorial bearings. A brass plate depicts Henry Clifford, 2nd Earl of Cumberland, with his brothers, Francis and Charles, with other kneeling figures.

Also worth noting are: the Sedilia of four seats with pointed trefoiled arches c.1350; the rood screen of 1533, with Perpendicular tracery; the font cover, being a very fine Jacobean piece; and in the north aisle a small opening perhaps leading originally to an anchorite's cell.

Skipton Castle to the Battery

From the Castle walk down by the Church and over the bridge to turn right and walk up Chapel Hill, left at the fork and on up to go over wall-stile by gateway. Walk up the hill to go over wall-stile by gate. The Battery is over on the left.

The Battery, Park Hill

The Battery is a small square raised mound sited on the summit of Park Hill, thought by some to be a cannon emplacement during the Civil War seige of Skipton Castle, given the find of a cannonball nearby. To the south, on Cock Hill, is another cannon emplacement. Here have been found a few cannonballs and a 17th century bronze spur, all on display in the Craven Museum. Some see Park Hill as the site of a Roman signal Station, contemporary with other presumed sites on Primrose Hill, Brogden, and Mellor Hill, above Ribchester.

The only Roman finds from the town of Skipton are 11 coins c.250-400, found in the Waller Hill Beck. These may have been offerings to the spirit of the Beck by travellers wishing a safe journey or other. The coins can be viewed in the Craven Museum, Skipton.

The Battery to Stirton Lane

Walk on down the hill to go over stiles and up onto By-pass. Cross the road and over fence-stile opposite. Cross the field to go over fence-stile. Walk directly over the Golf Course to go over corner stile in section of walling. Follow the wall around to go through stone gap-stile and follow wall on to go over stile by gate. Follow left-hand fence over on the left, down to go over the stile onto Brackenley Lane, left, and walk up the lane to the road junction. Cross the road and pass over stile opposite. Walk on directly to go over fence-stile (near electricity pole). Follow left-hand hedgerow then fence on to go over stile by gate onto road.

From here you have the choice of two pathways over Flasby Fell. The way to the left leads one through Crag Wood to the Enclosure, then on to view the Tumulus at Septeria Gill and on to Flasby. The way to the right is by far the better walk in my opinion, taking one over the high moor between Sharp Haw and Rough Haw with good views over Rylstone Fell.

ROUTE 1:
Crag Wood/Septeria Gill

Walk down the road to go over wall-stile at footpath sign on the right. Walk on to go through field gate. Follow left-hand hedge/fence on to go over fence-stile. Follow fence up to go over wall-stile by gate. Follow right-hand wall on to go over wall-stile by gate. Walk directly on, over the clough, to gateway into wood, walk up onto the forest trackway (*DO NOT TRY TO USE THE O.S. MAP TO FIND THE PATHWAY, YOU WON'T. As with other forestry enterprises, no respect is shown for Public Rights of Way*). Left, and walk down the track, right at the fork, and on up the hill to 'lay-by'. A track on the right leads up to the Enclosure and Sharp Haw.

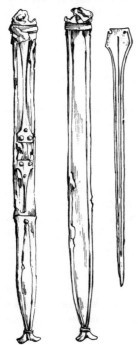

Sharp Haw Enclosure

Sharp Haw Enclosure is classified as a defensive, Iron Age, hill top site, built from and around a series of glacial eratics. The site probably served as a redoubt for the major pre-Roman settlement site at Gargrave, brought into use only in times of conflict when people and stock could be brought up onto the highlands for safety.

The Craven Museum displays two major finds from Flasby Fell: a Lower Bronze Age spearhead; and an Iron Age sword and scabbard, the sword is iron, the scabbard, bronze with a wooden lining.

IRON SWORD
IN BRONZE
SHEATH, FOUND
NEAR FLASBY,
WEST RIDING

Sharp Haw to Flasby

Return to the forest trackway and walk on down to the hairpin bend where you will find a footpath sign. Follow the path across the clearing to track by footpath sign. Follow the track down to go through gate into field. The bowl-barrow tumulus is over on the right (when opened it was found to contain an urn burial of Bronze Age date). Follow the track down, through a gate, and on down to Flasby.

ROUTE 2:
Sharp Haw/Rough Haw

Follow road on, around two corners and on to go through gateway on the left at third corner. Follow trackway on, through two gateways onto moor. Leave the trackway and walk up onto the moor, following poles to go through gateway.

To the left are the Craggs and the Iron Age Enclosure, in front rises the pike of Sharp Haw and on the right, Rough Haw. Over on the right Rylstone Fell dominates with Norton Tower and the War Memorial obelisk standing sentinel.

Cairn, Flasby Fell

A small stone cairn, on the rise to the north of Rough Haw SD. 963563, constructed of local gritstone boulders, the largest robbed for local walling, was excavated in 1964. It was found to rest upon an old turf-line with undisturbed podsoil section continuous beneath it. At its centre were found many burned flaggy grits, but no trace of any burial.

Sharp Haw to Flasby

Our path now goes between Sharp Haw and Rough Haw so follow the staked pathway on in the direction of Sharp Haw to veer sharply off the path to the right before the path ascends to the summit. Walk on to (in summer this meadow is covered in flax) go through field-gate in wall. Walk across the ling on a right-diagonal and down to go over stile by gate in wall below Rough Haw.

Walk on on a left-diagonal and follow the path down and over to the right of the clough, and on to go through field-gate in wall. Walk down the field to the far left-hand corner to join trackway via gate. Follow the trackway down into Flasby.

Flasby

Flasby is first recorded in the 1086 Domesday Survey, 'FLATEBI', a place-name of Old Norse origin meaning 'the farmstead of Flatr'. Today it is a small farming hamlet of half a dozen homesteads. One, of 17th century origin, displays a frontage of mullioned windows.

Flasby Hall

At the time of writing, Flasby Hall stands in ruin. It is an Italianate mansion of 1844, very restrained in detail except for the Victorian addition of a tower at the rear. In the grounds is a folly of a mediaeval round tower with a studded wooden door, very quaint.

On digging in the grounds of the Flasby Hall Estate for an enlargement of the house, I have been assured that many human bones and vestiges of an ancient chapel were discovered — another instance of the numerous domestic oratories once existing in Craven.

Flasby to the Canal at Gargrave

Turn left at the wall Post Box and walk down the lane to go over a fence-stile on the right at footpath sign. Walk up to go over next stile. Walk on a left diagonal to go over fence-stile (the ruin of Flasby Hall is on the left). Walk on to follow left-hand fence down to follow yellow marker-posts on to go up and through kissing-gate onto road. Left, and walk down the road, over the bridge (Eshton Hall is over on the right) and on to road junction. Go over the wall-stile on the left and cross field on a right diagonal to go over stile by gate.

Follow fence to the right to go over fence-stile (a magnificent view of Flasby Fell is to be had from here). Walk up the field veering slightly to the left, then directly on along the brow of the hill to go over stile by pine plantation on the left. Walk down to go over next stile. Cross the field directly to go over stile then footbridge and up onto the canal. Follow path down to the locks. Cross the footbridge onto the canal tow-path. Follow the tow-path on up to Gargrave.

GARGRAVE — THE GEOLOGY

Gargrave is situated in the Craven Lowlands, an area of Lower Carboniferous limestones built of a series of E.N.E./W.S.W. folds, prominent amongst these are the Clitheroe-Skipton and Slaidburn anticlines. The north east end of the latter is crossed by the Craven Faults; the North Craven Fault disconnects the reef limestones of Cracoe from the more northern facies, the Middle Craven Fault separating the reef limestones of Elbolton and Thorpe Kail from that of Swinden and Butterhaw and the South Craven Fault dividing up into two faults which pass through Winterburn and Gargrave respectively.

From Malham to Bell Busk and Gargrave there is a deep mass of impure, layered limestone with frequent bands of calcareous shale, the whole being greatly contorted, denuded and obscured by glacial drift. In Airedale, however, there is only slight drift comprised of two types: a boulder clay fill of scratched limestone blocks and a superjacent deposit of sand and gravel.

The triangle of land between Clitheroe, Long Preston and Skipton is occupied by drumlins that have blocked the valley of the pre-glacial River Aire to the north-west of Gargrave. At numerous points moraines cross the Aire Valley, the nearest to Gargrave being at Cononley. A late glacial lake, seven miles long, formed to the north of this moraine. It silted up with a great depth of layered clay and fine sand forming a glacial lake flat which now forms part of the flood plain of the River Aire.

If you are making a lunch stop at Gargrave, then may I suggest the Masons Arms opposite the church, as a quiet watering hole. The Swan, in the centre of the village, is also worth a visit.

Canal at Gargrave to Skipton

Follow the tow-path all the way down to Skipton town centre.

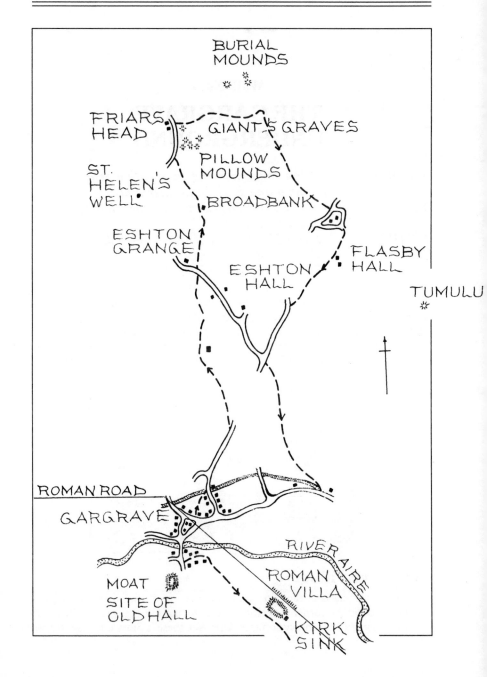

Walk No.5

THE GARGRAVE UNDERGROUND

7½ miles	*A few hours morning walk with a visit to the Church and Kirk Sink after lunch.*
LUNCH:	*The Masons Arms, opposite the Church, or the Old Swan.*
START:	*Swan Hotel in the centre of the village.*
MAP:	*O.S. SD 85/95 PATHFINDER SERIES.*

A curious title for a walk you may think, but considering that the majority of sites that we shall visit today are in this present age only earthen humps, bumps and ditches, then it is most appropriate. The walk leads us through estate parkland up onto the green pastures of Scarnber Hill to return by way of ancient green lanes via Flasby to Gargrave and an exploration of that lovely village.

Gargrave Village

Our 'field trip' starts at the Old Swan in the centre of the village. From here we walk around the corner into North Street to find our eyes greeted by a very pleasant row of 17th century cottages. Opposite these is Story's House. Robert

Story, schoolmaster and poet, had this house built for him in 1828 by Mathew Wilson Esq of Eshton Hall. Further up North Street we find a 17th century house, with a full mullioned windowed frontage. The doorhead of the house bears the date 1690, with the initials G.S.

The Old Swan, Gargrave, to Brockabank

Come out of the pub, left, and into North Street. Follow pathway at 'cyclist sign' opposite to Eshton Road locks. Cross the bridge and walk up Eshton Road to go left over wall-stile by gate. Cross the field on a right-diagonal following line of trees to go over fence-stile. Walk up the hill on a left-diagonal to enter wood by gate in fence. Follow the pathway through the wood to leave by kissing-gate. Cross the field on a left-diagonal to go over fence-stile and on to go over next fence-stile. Walk up to enter roadway via wall-stile. Left, and over the wall-stile opposite. Cross field to go over stile in far left corner. Walk down the ridge line to go over stile onto trackway. Follow trackway down, over bridge (notice lime kiln and quarry over on the right) and on up to Brockabank.

Brockabank

Set amid a gorgeous cottage garden is the splendid mullioned pile of Brockabank. For the most part this is a 17th century house, but some parts of the structure go back to the 16th century. Below Brockabank, by the road leading from Eshton House to Friars Head can be found St. Helen's Well.

St. Helen's Well, Eshton

St. Helen's Well at Eshton is said to possess healing properties for eye-diseases and a number of smaller ailments. If you place your arms into the waters and search around you will soon feel the head and bust of a stone image of St. Helen, placed here within the depths in some ancient time.

In the 18th century a cross-shaft resembling those in Whalley (Lancs) churchyard was discovered opposite the well. Alas, I do not know its present whereabouts, perhaps it is one of those now to be seen in Gargrave Church.

The practice of regarding water, and in particular a well, as having sacred and healing qualities is well attested among the Celtic peoples. Holy wells have their origins in the pre-English period and many occur on a number of Roman sites in West and North Yorkshire. With the coming of Christianity the pagan deities to whom the wells were dedicated were converted and replaced by a Christian saint — St. Helen was especially popular in those early times.

St Helen was the mother of Constantine the Great and said to be of Northern British origin, an ancester of Coel Hen Godebog — the post-Roman overlord of Northern Britain who came down in legend as 'Old King Cole'. After her conversion to Christianity she made an energetic and devout pilgrimage to Jerusalem, and founded several churches in Palestine.

Her popularity began to crystallize about seventy years after her death after the story went round that she was privileged to discover the cross of Christ on the site of the Passion. She is usually depicted wearing a crown and holding a long T-cross.

Lime Kilns

One of the most common industrial features in the Lancashire and Yorkshire limestone regions is the limekiln. The majority of farmers with limestone on their land had their own field-kiln which they could fire up in the quieter autumn season.

The kiln would be strategically placed near a limestone outcrop so that it required the minimum carriage of the bulkiest raw material. Notice the kiln below Brockabank and its adjacent quarried outcrop.

The lime burning contributed to the recovery and improvement of the rough hill pastures of the Dales, partly through simply spreading to neutralize soil acids, and partly by means of 'paring and burning'. This latter method was practiced throughout the north.

The section of ground to be recovered would be first walled in, then the sod was 'pared' off in turfs. These turfs were then stacked up to dry out, then burnt, and the potash-rich ashes spread over the ground, followed by a heavy liming. This new ground would then be ploughed, and if not at too high an elevation, cropped with turnips followed by oats, and finally, after two or three years, sown down to grass. The cropping with turnips and oats would give enough profit to pay for the winning of the ground. A lot of good ground in the valley heads was made in this way.

Brockabank to Friars Head

Walk past the front of the house to go over stile by gate. Follow left-hand wall on and down to cross field onto trackway (notice the lime kiln over on the right). Follow trackway to roadway and on to Friars Head.

Friars Head, Winterburn

Friars Head above Eshton, in Airedale, is one of the finest of all the 17th century houses in the Dales. The front is symmetrical, of two storeys with four gables each with even bay windows on each floor of six-light transomed. In the gables are three-light windows with ogee heads under truncated ogee hood-moulds. The porch in the second bay has as an entrance with three-centred arch on moulded responds. To the rear are two slightly projecting wings with an array of plainly mullioned windows.

The house stands upon the site of a grange of Furness Abbey whose tenants at Friars Head were the Procter family. A Thomas Procter held the farm of Furness Abbey at the time of his death in 1507. The tenancy devolved upon his son Stephen, then in 1530 we find Stephen's son, Gabrial, living there as steward and bailiff of Furness Abbey estates here and in Winterburn.

After the Dissolution, Stephen Proctor, his son born at Friars Head in 1562, enriched himself by trade and investment and rebuilt the house in its present form around c.1600.

In 1596 he purchased the remaining estates of Fountains Abbey from the heirs of Sir Richard Gresham, then built Fountains Hall, the magnificent mansion that adjoins the Abbey today. Upon comparing the two houses, both buildings have a great deal in common and it is obvious that Friars Head had been the prototype for Fountains Hall.

Giants' Graves, Pillow Mounds

The Giants' Graves stand to the east of Friars Head on the hillside above the road. Seven rectangular mounds can be clearly defined, they are 15ft. wide and between 32ft and 42ft long. The correct term for these earthworks is Pillow Mounds. These ditched barrows have been the subject of much speculation, and in the past have been referred to as bracken stock bottoms, but now they are generally regarded as being artificial rabbit warrens.

The rabbit, introduced by the Normans, has been a source of food and fur since the late 12th century, and at times has been encouraged for these things. Warrens are frequently referred to in mediaeval documents, but their exact form, apart that some were fenced to facilitate trapping, does not seem to be known.

Also near Friars Head is a faintly discernable rectangle of 80ft by 90ft having a tumulus close to its east side.

Near the summit of Banks Hill, to the north east of Friars Head are three ancient mounds. Excavations in the mounds have found sherds of an urn/beaker and burnt fragments of human bone. The Craven Museum Catalogue ascribes a Bronze Age origin.

Friars Head to Howson Laithe

From the front entrance gate walk up the road to go through gate on the right at footpath sign. Follow left-hand wall up, through gateway and on to go through next gateway. Cross the field on a right-diagonal to go through a field gate. Follow left-hand wall to corner gates (from here we can view the rugged skyline to the north of Skipton. Norton Tower, on the left, Flasby Fell and then Sharp Haw are all laid before us — a magnificent sight). At the corner walk down the field then head up the steep banking to go through gate in far wall. Follow left-hand wall on, through two gates and on down to the road.

HOWSON
LAITHE

Howson Laithe

The cottage at Howson Laithe displays a dated doorhead of 1683, with the initials R.M.O. The name 'laithe' is Old Norse 'hlaoa', and means 'a barn'.

Howson Laithe to Flasby

Walk down the road opposite into the hamlet of Flasby.

A description of Flasby can be found in the walk 'Craven Strongholds'.

Eshton Hall

Eshton Hall was built in around 1826 by the architect George Webster of Kendal for Sir Mathew Wilson. It is now a retirement home, and the Wilson family now lives at Eshton House, a solid Georgian edifice a little further up the road.

Flasby to Gargrave Church

Turn left at the wall post-box and walk down the lane to go over fence-stile on the right. Walk up to go over next stile. Walk on a left-diagonal to go over fence-stile (the deserted Flasby Hall is over on the left). Walk on to follow left-hand fence down to follow yellow marker-posts on to go up and through kissing-gate onto road. Left, and walk down the road, over the bridge (Eshton Hall is over on the right) and on to the road junction. Go over the wall-stile on the left and cross the field on a right-diagonal to go over stile by gate. Follow fence to the right to go over fence-stile.

Walk up the field veering slightly to the left, then directly on along the brow of the hill to follow line of old trackway to go over stile by pine plantation on the left. Walk down to go over next stile. Cross the field to go over stile then footbridge and up onto the canal. Walk down to the locks and over footbridge. Follow the canal up to Gargrave. Make your way from the main street to the road bridge over the River Aire and follow the road on to the Parish Church. The Masons Arms is over on the right. Notice the old posting box set into the side of the inn wall.

St. Andrew's Church

The present church is of the rebuilding of 1859, built of the reddish stone quarried from Sharp Haw, and very typical of that time. The tower, however, is a survivor from the previous edifice and bears a date A.D. MDXXI (1521). The church itself has a very ancient foundation.

In 1313, Henry de Percy released all his rights in tithes of Stainton and granted the advowson of Gargrave and all its chapels (Coniston Cold etc.) to Sawley Abbey in return for the payment of 80 marks. From this time the Abbey of Sawley held authority at Gargrave until the Reformation.

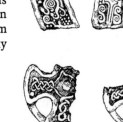

Inside the church are relics of pre-Conquest worship: sited at the rear of the nave, by the south door, are fragments from four Anglo-Scandinavian standing crosses. Animal figures and other abstracts decorate the faces of these stones. These were found in the fabric of the old church when it was pulled down in order to build the present one.

Many early churches were built upon Celtic pre-Christian religious sites, and this may have been the case at Gargrave; in the churchyard are the stumps of three old lime trees, cut down when they became decayed and unsafe. It is said that they grew on part of the old boundary, which was circular and could have joined up to the curve on the north-west corner.

The Manor of Gargrave

Gargrave in 1284 was a split manor consisting of two knights fees being of 18 carucates in extent of which 10½ were in the fee of the Castle of Skipton and 7½ of the fee of Percy.

The reason for such a division was to purposely break up the administrative centre of the Celtic Cantrev of Craven once the Caput of Pabo Post Prydein, great, great grandson of Coel Hen Godebog who came down to our time in legend as 'Old King Cole'. But more of these Celtic Heroes later when we come to look at Kirk Sink.

Gargrave, once a market town, was the ancient central parish of Craven. During the Mediaeval period its fertile countryside provided wheat, beans, oats and barley for the convent at Sawley whose fortunes slumped after the devastating Scots raid on the area in 1338 when King David led his army on a raid into England.

Part of the Scottish army under David's nephew, William fitz Duncan, was detached into Yorkshire. With great carnage they laid waste the province of Craven with fire and sword. Old charters inform us that William fitz Duncan had already acquired the district north of the River Ribble along with Craven by his marriage to Alice, one of the co-heiresses of William Meschin, the brother of the infamous Ranulf of Chester.

It seems likely that he was being kept out of his inheritance, perhaps by Ilbert de Lacy, lord of the honor of Clitheroe, who held lands in Craven.

The Percy fee was to the south of the River Aire along with the advowson of the church which was in the Percys hands until 1313. The moated site known as the Garris was the site of the manor house relating to the Percy fee. In 1255 John de Longvilliers died seised of the manor of Gargrave, and in 1280 the free warren was granted to Geoffry de Nevil. Gargrave gave name and residence to a marital family who bore lozengery as their arms showing dependence to the ancient Neviles of Gargrave.

Of this family was Sir Robert Gargrave who became Governor of Pontusom in France under Henry V. His son, Sir Thomas, was Master of the Forests and Marshal of the English Army under Henry VI at the Siege of Orleans where he was slain. Their family seat was the Garris.

The moated site known as Garris, named after the Gargraves of Gargrave, stands in the field adjoining the old National Church School being a clearly defined system of moated Hall site, mounds and ditches.

The site has never been the subject of archaeological excavation, the only find from the site was the chance discovery of an ancient purse in c.1800. The frame is made of brass with inlaid steel lettering, which reads: AVE MARIA GACIA PLEA DOMINS TECUM CREDO IN DEOM PATRAN OM. Whitaker, in his 'History of Craven', states that a date for the purse could not be later than Henry II, (1154-1189).

Nearby stands the mullion fronted Garris House, a 17th century survivor of this half of the village, that along with Paget Hall across the way and a doorhead of 1670 on a restored house to the north of the church are for the most part all that remain of that period.

One notable person from the Percy fee of Gargrave was Robert of Gargrave, monk of Newminster, near Morpeth. About 1147, Robert sent out three colonies of monks from Newminster to found other abbeys, one of which was to be at Sawley, near Clitheroe. Robert was later canonised as St. Robert of Newminster.

To the north of the River Aire was the Romill fee that later came under the fee of Skipton Castle, seat of the Clifford family. The site of the manor house relating to this fee was situated behind North Street beyond Old Hall Fold.

This moated site was the subject of an archaeological excavation between the years 1977 to 1981, a summary of the findings are recorded here:

The excavation revealed the existence of a complex Mediaeval seignorial site with evidence of intensive occupation during the 13th and 14th centuries. This consisted originally of a moated, domestic site with a number of ancillary buildings. The moat was short lived having been filled in and built over by the early 14th century.

Evidence was also found of the living quarters being moved to Old Hall Fold during the 14th century, after which date some of the ancillary buildings surrounding the site of the old manor house remained in use, although these too were down by the end of the century. After that time the site was in part cultivated and in part used to erect new ancillary building to the farmhouse in Old Hall Fold.

Along with a great amount of mediaeval pottery etc., a number of much earlier objects were discovered. These included flint artefacts dating from the Early Bronze Age and several sherds of 4th century Roman pottery, but no sign of human activity on the site prior to the early 13th century.

The Masons Arms to Kirk Sink

Follow the lane down by the side of the churchyard and on into farmyard (it is from the farmer here that one gains permission to walk on the field-site of Kirk Sink). Follow the trackway on to Kirk Sink, on the left in the field just before the house.

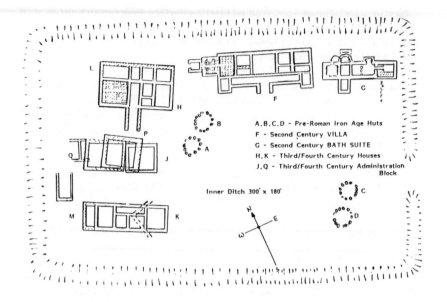

A,B,C,D - Pre-Roman Iron Age Huts
F - Second Century VILLA
G - Second Century BATH SUITE
H,K - Third/Fourth Century Houses
J,Q - Third/Fourth Century Administration Block

Inner Ditch 300' x 180'

Kirk Sink

Around 1740 drainage ditches were cut through the field on which we now stand. During the work a building with an apsidal projection was discovered. This was assumed to be a former church and so came about the name Kirk Sink.

At the same time a mosaic pavement was also seen and the site regarded as a Roman Villa with an early church/temple on the complex.

In 1908, after the partial excavation of the Roman Fort at Elslack, Dr Francis Villy made an initial examination of the Kirk Sink site to determine the nature of the site and any possible association with Elslack. He concluded that the final stage of the series of buildings on the site were residential, and thought that further work on the site would reveal other buildings.

During the years 1968 to 1975 the site was further subjected to archaeological excavations under the direction of Brian Hartley from Leeds University.

A villa building complete with hypocaust, furnace room and mosaic flooring was uncovered. Sadly the design of the mosaic could not be reconstructed entirely. Two houses were seen to have tessellated floors and painted wall-plaster. On the north east corner of the site stood the bath house whose general plan included a dressing room (Apodyterium), a Frigidarium with an apsed cold water-bath projecting to the north. On the west side of the Frigidarium was a hot room (Laconicum) with a pillared hypocaust. The building was seen to have been added to and altered a number of times.

Finds from the site included amounts of Samian ware, good table glass, a silvered bronze spoon, a bronze terret-ring, a trumpet brooch and two cheese presses. All going to prove that here once stood a place of great distinction, the seat of the Roman Craven overlord.

The villa site was seen to have been established on an earlier native Brigantian Iron Age site consisting of a number of round huts. These had been constructed with turf walls with inner daub plasterwork, being c.17 feet in diameter with a central post. These appear to have been in use up to the second half of the second century.

The site can be interpreted as one surrounded by rich farmland and pasture, the estate centre of a Brigante chieftain of some note, overlord of the Celtic cantrev of Cravenshire, as these lands would come to be known later. The villa would be gifted to this ruling dynasty for their co-operation in subjugating the tribal clans in this border Pennine area.

I hand over to Tacitus to explain this process of social change:

"To induce a people, hitherto scattered and uncivilised, and therefore prone to fight, to grow pleasurably inured to peace and ease, Agricola gave private encouragement and official assistance to the building of temples, public squares and private mansions.

"He praised the keen and scolded the slack, and competition for honour proved as effective as compulsion. Furthermore, he trained the sons of chiefs in the liberal arts and expressed a preference for British natural ability over the trained skill of the Gauls.

"The result was that in place of distaste for the Latin language came a passion to command it. In the same way, our national dress came into favour and the toga was everywhere to be seen.

"And so the Britons were gradually led on to the amenities that make vice agreeable — arcades, baths and sumptuous banquets. They spoke of such novelties as 'civilisation' when really they were only a feature of their enslavement." (AGRICOLA, 21).

Tacitus here is referring to the tribes of lowland Britain, but the same trick would be applied, but perhaps to a lesser extent given their remoteness, to the confederated tribes within Brigantia.

I suspect that the village site for the Kirk Sink villa was astride the ford in the centre of the modern settlement of Gargrave. After the withdrawal of Roman administration from the region the villa homestead would fall into disrepair and become defunct. The overlord reverting to tribal ways and customs of a Celtic peoples.

The ruling group probably positioned their seat opposite the church on the 'Garris' moated site. The redoubt in times of danger would have been the hill fort enclosure on Sharp Haw, a position that gives one commanding views over the Gargrave district.

Three roads have been detected leading from the Kirk Sink site. An eastern exit leads in the direction of Stirton, one runs northward to cross the River Aire and another heads towards the church and Aire Bridge. A section of this last road was located some six feet below ground level in the farmyard of Paget Hall, this lines up to a well paved roadway crossing the River Aire some fifteen yards below the present bridge. At a point some twelve yards below the bridge were discovered about ten wooden supports in pairs from a very ancient bridge.

Craven is an area situated in the north-western corner of the old West Riding of Yorkshire, a name that is derived from the Celtic word 'craf', meaning garlic. The three rivers of the Ribble, Aire and Wharfe originate in the northern watersheds of this ancient shire.

As to it once being an independent British state, as yet, there is no conclusive evidence unlike the neighbouring Elmet. The evidence for the existence of the kingdom of Elmet consists of a number of literary references, its survival as an administrative body late enough to be recorded in the 7th century Mercian Tribal Hidage, and the occurence of the affix "in Elmet" in mediaeval place-names.

The name is mentioned by the Celtic poets Aneirin and Taliesin, and the reference in the 'Historia Brittonum' to Edwin of Northumbria's expulsion of Ceretic from Elmet in 617 proves conclusively that Elmet was an independent British kingdom. Had this reference failed to survive, the evidence for its independent status would have been no better than that for Craven.

In our Historical Introduction we argue that the area known as Craven was once a Celtic cantrev, a minor kingdom within a greater realm once held by Pabo Post Prydein.

I would go further and suggest that Pabo had his chief caput here at Gargrave. This can at best be only a speculation, but given its prominent position astride a number of important and ancient trade routes and the fact that the Romans deemed it an important site from which to administer the region, not to mention the importance of an early church here, make Gargrave a strong contender for that role.

The unfolding historical landscapes that these walks explore, here and within companion volumes, will, we hope, add more weight to the argument and lead to a reappraisal of the district of Craven (and other central northern areas that once formed Brigantia) in the post-Roman period.

Retrace your footsteps back to the village of Gargrave, and if time permits give the village a full exploration.

The Old Mill

The old mill at Gargrave, now used for storage, was one of the first in the district to introduce power looms. The locals, fearing the reduction in labour, came together as an armed mob and attacked Mason's mill and destroyed the power looms.

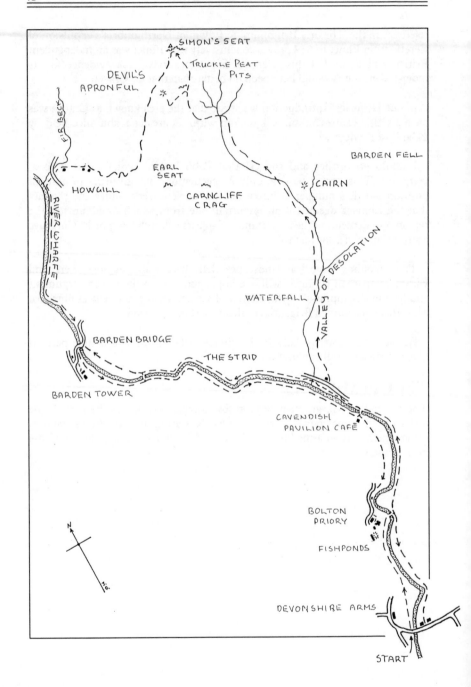

Walk No.6

CANONS' FISHPONDS AND DEVIL'S APRONFUL

13 miles and 6½ miles, 7 and 3 hours.

MAP: *O.S. SE 05/15 PATHFINDER SERIES,*
                or O.S. LEISURE 10, S. Yorkshire Dales.
LUNCH: *Barden Tower Café.*
START: *Bolton Bridge or Bolton Abbey.*

The longer walk starts from Bolton Bridge and climbs up to Simon's Seat, via 'The Valley of Desolation', to return by following the Wharfe down from Howgill. The shorter walk starts from the Priory and follows the right bank of the river up to the Strid and on to Barden Tower to return on the opposite bank.

Both paths go through the Chatsworth Estate, some of which are not public rights of way and are subject to a small toll, or are part of the Barden Moor and Fell Access Agreement between North Yorkshire County Council and the Duke of Devonshire. Under this agreement, the Duke has opened a large proportion of the open land on his estate to the public, subject to certain by-laws that require compliance with the 'Country Code' and that dogs are not allowed on the areas or paths covered by the agreement.

The walk itself is one of the most beautiful and famous in the Southern Dales, remarkable for its lushness and greenery in the summer months and for its blaze of autumn colour. The clarity gained in the winter months adds a new dimension to the ramble, all this to say nothing of the remarkable architecture to be dwelt upon, adds up to a truely great day out.

Bolton Bridge to Bolton Priory

Pass through the little gate by the side of the bridge and follow the 'DALES WAY' marked footpath upriver to Bolton Priory.

Bolton Priory

I will not try to emulate the fine description of the Priory and its location
given by Ruskin in 1856. Nor can our
drawing match those romantic images
of Turner, Palmer or Cole. Enough to
say that the vistas laid out in sweeps of
the Wharfe bring out that simple faith
in a village England so long ago burnt
within our soul.

Bolton Priory was founded in 1151
by Alicia de Romilly. Her mother had
endowed a priory for the black-robed
Augustinian Canons at Embsay, near
Skipton, in 1120. Alicia transferred
them to Bolton. Of the canons' church
much remains: the western section is
now roofed and is now the parish

Doorway—Bolton Abbey.

church, the eastern section rests in a picturesque ruinous state, and sections of the living quarters are made more eloquent by the result of excavations. The house of the Dukes of Devonshire, Bolton Hall, opposite the tower, contains in its middle the gatehouse of the priory.

The original tower was on the crossing of the transepts. The western tower of 1520 is unfinished and adjoins the original west front of the church. The projecting stones inside show that the two were never joined together. The west front is magnificent and cannot fail to inspire, why they ever wished to cover it up is beyond me. The workmanship is in the Early English style of the mid-13th century, highly ornate. Once inside the nave of the Priory, now the parish church, we are greeted by a Gregorian Chant performed by monks

Chancel, Bolton Abbey.

whose strains fill the air with quiet mystic prayer. A number of good guide books are on sale at the back of the church along with other related objects. A book on the history and architecture of the Priory is well worth the purchase.

The finest parts of the building are to be seen amid the ruins of the former chancel. Here in the western section we have the Canons' seats with intersected Late Norman blank arcading and round-headed arches on scalloped capitals and waterleaf capitals of various designs. The sedilia remains, with seats for the four priests who conducted the mass. Nearby an arched doorway leads to the crypt in which members of the Cillord family of Skipton Castle were once buried.

Bolton Priory was suppressed in 1539, but the last Prior, Richard Moone, walled off the nave for the villagers to use as a parish church as it remains today.

To the south east of the Priory, behind the 17th century Tithe Barn, can be found the Prior's Fish Ponds, once an important source of food for the priory community.

Bolton Priory to Simon's Seat

Cross the footbridge below the Priory and follow the trackway on along the woodland slopes to roadway and across the ford. Left, and rejoin the footpath on to the Cavendish Pavilion bridge and on through gates along the riverside path to go over stile. Take the up-hill path on the right to roadway and walk on up the road to take the path on the right at 1 in 8 sign.

Pass through the gate and follow the path on, through gate and on to go down and on to the waterfall (the path on the right before you go down the river bank takes you above and beyond the waterfall to cross the river by a footbridge, this way should be taken if you are not sure footed or have children with you). Climb up the path to cross the river above the waterfall.

Follow the path on into the Valley of Desolation (here gritstone boulders gape out gauntly through the bracken covered slopes) and onto Public Access path, then on up to enter wood via stile.

Follow path in front of you on up through the wood and onto the moor via gate. Follow the well defined track directly on to cross Great Agill Beck and on up the eastern side of the clough, passing the stone seat and on to go over the head of the clough and on to the fortress rocks of Simon's Seat.

Simon's Seat

The location and the walk up is akin to a Scottish grouse moor, with the ling covered hillsides and bracken decked cloughs and here and there the mountain ash standing forth. Gritstones gape from all sides, some rising to massive fortress type formations, their sides scarred by the passing of the glacier.

After the retreat of the ice mastiff these hills were colonised by beach and hazel leaving the great oaks and birch to cover the lower slopes and valley floor. Cave bear, wolf, leopard, elk and Auroch hunted and grazed with the seasons.

When man arrived he settled the high tops — the Wharfedale Neolithic floor. This 'floor' is today preserved in the peat deposits of the upland moors. The mean temperature was 2 deg. C higher than it is today, which allowed farming and settlement to exist at far higher elevations than today.

As the climate became cooler and wetter, in combination with the artificial clearance of forest in the upland areas which led to a gradual leaching of soil nutrients, sphagnum moss and cotton grass colonised the uplands resulting in the blanket of peat which is so widespread today. This combination of factors led Neolithic man from his original upland settlements down to the lower levels, a process which became complete during the Bronze Age.

Remains of man's passing can still be detected in the landscape here today. To the south west of Simon's Seat is a large cairn, known as "The Devil's Apronful", and above Hudson Gill Beck is an ancient cairn. To the north are numerous cup-marked rocks, stone circles and many settlement sites. The cairns represent large living huts and burial sites, and many more are to be found scattered over Barden Moor.

Excavations in the Truckle Peat Pits, to the south just below Simon's Seat on Barden Fell, have revealed flint microliths that occur in a layer of grey sand underlying about 8ft of peat (see diagram over page). Near the base of the peat is a 'forest' layer of birch stumps and tree trunks. Above this is a dark brown peat, followed by light brown fibrous peat then by more recent sphagnum moss and heather peats. The sand in which the flints occur is the product of the weathering of rock-head and boulder clay during the warm and dry Boreal period (see Summary of Subdivisions chart over page).

These small worked flints, known as pygmy flints or microliths are the

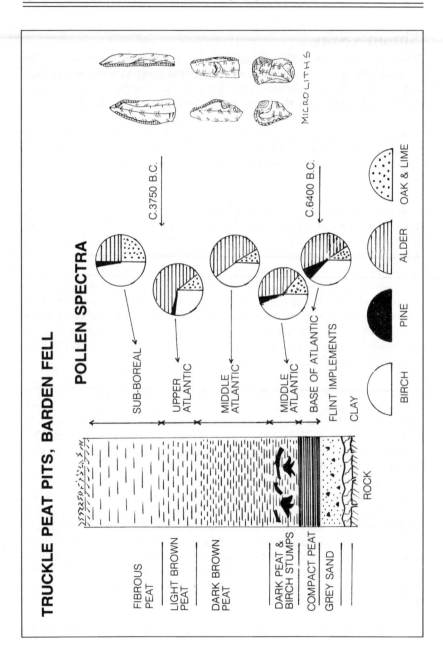

SUMMARY of SUBDIVISIONS, CLIMATIC & ENVIRONMENTAL CHANGES
for the NORTH of ENGLAND in the POST-GLACIAL PERIOD

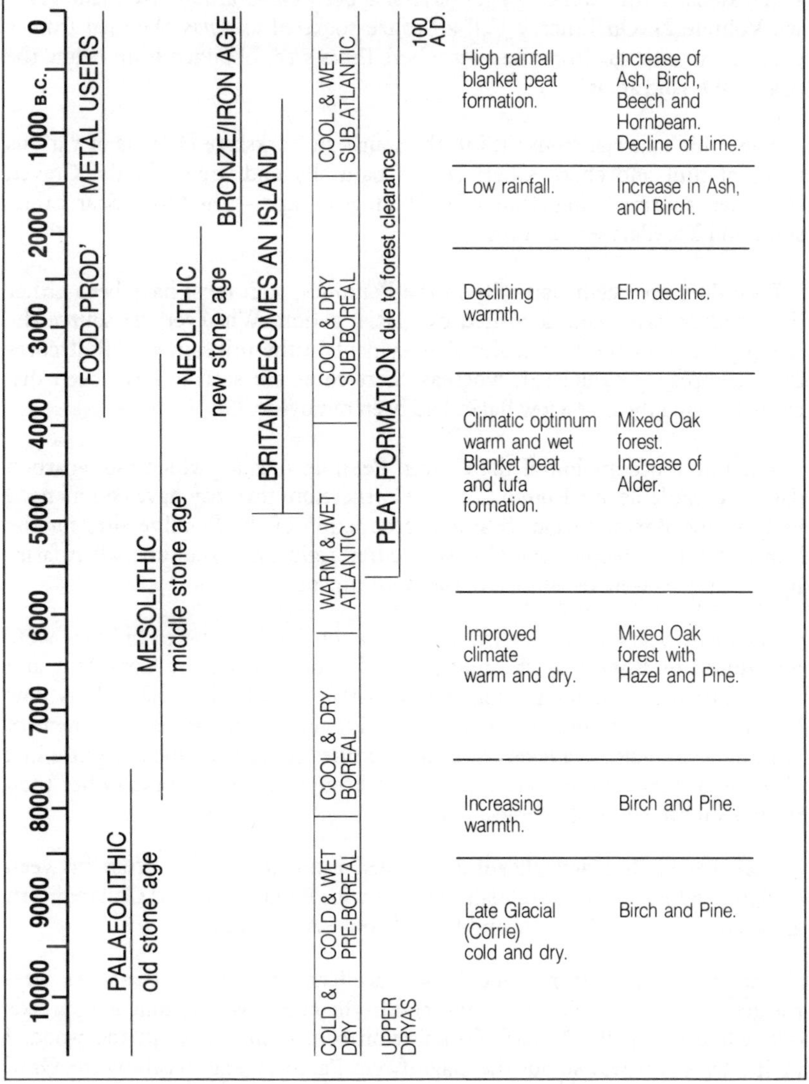

Time scale (left axis): 0 / 1000 B.C. / 2000 / 3000 / 4000 / 5000 / 6000 / 7000 / 8000 / 9000 / 10000, with 100 A.D. at top.

Cultural subdivisions:
- PALAEOLITHIC old stone age
- MESOLITHIC middle stone age
- FOOD PROD'
- METAL USERS
- NEOLITHIC new stone age
- BRONZE/IRON AGE
- BRITAIN BECOMES AN ISLAND

Climatic periods:
- UPPER DRYAS — COLD & DRY
- COLD & WET PRE-BOREAL
- COOL & DRY BOREAL
- WARM & WET ATLANTIC
- COOL & DRY SUB BOREAL
- COOL & WET SUB ATLANTIC

PEAT FORMATION due to forest clearance

(reading top = recent → bottom = earliest)	Rainfall / Climate	Vegetation
(100 A.D. – top)	High rainfall blanket peat formation.	Increase of Ash, Birch, Beech and Hornbeam. Decline of Lime.
	Low rainfall.	Increase in Ash, and Birch.
	Declining warmth.	Elm decline.
	Climatic optimum warm and wet Blanket peat and tufa formation.	Mixed Oak forest. Increase of Alder.
	Improved climate warm and dry.	Mixed Oak forest with Hazel and Pine.
	Increasing warmth.	Birch and Pine.
(10000 – bottom)	Late Glacial (Corrie) cold and dry.	Birch and Pine.

result of flint knapping/working and are observed in the form of cores, scrapers, blades, etc.

Other sites from this period have been found on Rylstone Fell and Embsay Fell (extensive flint-working sites have also been found around Malham Tarn, see Volume 2). On Embsay Fell a bronze socketed axe was obtained from a peat cutting, not far from the sites where flints were obtained from below the peat in the sand areas.

The lithic material from sites in the southern Yorkshire Dales is of various types of flint and chert. Chert occurs naturally and widely in the Craven Pennines, sources being strata of Carboniferous age — the Great Scar Limestone and Yoredale series of rocks.

Flint does not occur naturally in the Pennines, so it must have been either imported or have been deposited by glacial action. Whatever the source the scarcity value of the flint material is evident in the utilisation of flint cores until completely exhausted, whereas chert cores are seen to have been discarded often only after a few flakes had been removed.

The initial occupation of the Craven Pennine sites for which radio-carbon dates are available are around 6250 B.C., therefore this may have commenced early in the Boreal period. Seasonal occupation of the Pennine sites for the hunter/gatherer peoples would have occured right up to the time when farming techniques were developed in the Neolithic period.

For many years archaeologists have thought that farming techniques were introduced to Britain by the migration of peoples from the Continent and their settlement and integration into a British Mesolithic society. It is now held that changing climatic conditions facilitated the natural development of farming technology to a level were communities could permanently settle in a given area. Innovations were introduced through trade networks rather than the mass movements of peoples/folk.

Leaf-shaped flint arrowheads have been estimated to date from between c.2340-1550 B.C. These are mainly found with Food Vessel and Collared Urn associations — late Neolithic and Early Bronze Age contexts.

The views gained from Simon's Seat are fantastic. Over to the south west the great bulk of Pendle dominates, and in the near west Rylstone fell spreads out, while on up the Wharfe Grassington comes into view. In the wooded ravine across the way stands the magnificent Parcevall Hall recalling the Grail

Knight of Arthurian Myth. Parcevall was in fact a native of Brigantia —
Peredur, nephew of Urien et Rheged, and one time king of York.

Many walkers take the 'Dalehead' footpath to Howgill from here that de-
scends quickly to the valley floor along which they follow the long lane into
Howgill. I much prefer the route here as it remains on the high ground as long
as possible allowing one to maintain the magnificent views over the southern
Dales a little longer.

Simon's Seat to Barden Bridge

*Follow the south-easterly signed 'Howgill' path down and over the moor to
enter forest trackway and on to go over stile. Follow track down through the
wood to Howgill Lane via gate. Walk on and down the pathway by the side of
the buildings and on to the roadway. Cross over and walk down the trackway
opposite to follow the River Wharfe down, over stiles, to the roadway at
Barden Bridge.*

Barden Bridge

Barden Bridge was built in 1659 and repaired in 1676. It has three segmental
arches and recesses over the cutwaters. A stone on the bridge informs us that
'THIS BRIDGE WAS REPARED AT THE CHARGE OF THE WHOLE
WEST RIDING 1676'.

Barden Bridge to Barden Tower

*Cross the bridge and walk up the road and around to go over wall-stile on left
and on up the path to Barden Tower. After visiting return to the bridge.*

Barden Tower

The Tower was originally one of six lodges for Forest keepers in the late 11th
century and became the property of the Clifford family in 1310. The impressive tower house was built by the 10th Lord Clifford, Henry the 'Shepherd
Lord' (1485-1523), and restored and added to by Lady Anne Clifford in
1658-9. Though the house is in ruins its position in Wharfedale is exquisite. A
large, tall house of three storeys, it is subdivided into various apartments.

To the south is the Priest's Cottage and Chapel, built by Lady Anne Clifford, being typical of 17th century building. The nave and chancel are one and
the windows are tall and mullioned having lights with four-centred heads. The
tower, with porch under, has an outer stair leading to the upper floors.

In 1748 the Tower became the property of the Dukes of Devonshire and is now in the care of the Trustees of the Chatsworth Settlement. It has been in a ruinous condition since c.1800, having not been lived in since Lady Clifford's death in 1676.

Light lunches and teas are served on most days from the Priest's Cottage and Chapel, making for a good halfway stop within a very romantic setting.

Across the way is the Bunkbarn, a comfortable self-catering facility in a converted Dales barn. It accommodates up to 20 people in rooms catering for 2, 4, 6 & 8 people. The kitchen area is fully equipped and the site is an ideal base for walking holidays in the Wharfedale area.

Strid Wood

A whole range of nature's delights can be found in these exciting woods and a stroll along some of the selected trails is fascinating. From the rocks in the shallows of the Wharfe the Dipper can be seen plying his busy trade, and in the variety of woodland squirrels and rabbits freely go about their day. As the river narrows and widens it provides varied habitats to the riverside animal and plant life. A very rewarding woodland walk.

Barden Bridge to Bolton Priory

Pass over the stile on the east side of the bridge and follow the path on down through Strid Wood to the Cavendish Pavilion and on to the Priory.

Bolton Priory to Bolton Bridge

Cross the footbridge below the Priory and walk up to take the path on the right, along the top of the headland to go over stile and on across the steep cliff (this is one of the best vantage points to gain magnificent views over the Priory and the great sweep of the woods) to go over next stile. Follow hedge and fence downhill to go over stile to right of field gate. Walk on to go through field-gate and on taking a track which ascends above the woodland ahead to go over stile. Follow the cliff top around to descend towards the farm to go over stile and across a paddock onto the main road. Right, and walk on to Bolton Bridge.

Bolton Priory to Barden Bridge, via The Strid

Cross the footbridge below the Priory and follow the trackway on along the woodland slopes to roadway and across the ford. Left, and rejoin the footpath on to the Cavendish Pavilion bridge and on through gates along the riverside path to go over stile. Follow the lower riverside path on through the woods to the Strid. Follow the path on up river, passing the castellated aquaduct bridge on to Barden Bridge.

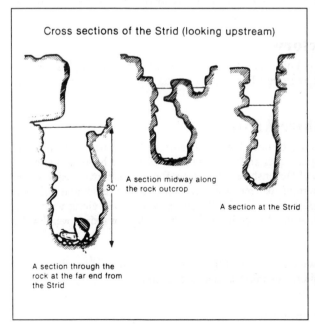

Cross sections of the Strid (looking upstream)

30'

A section midway along the rock outcrop

A section at the Strid

A section through the rock at the far end from the Strid

The Strid

Legend informs us that Alicia de Romilly transferred the Canons from Embsay to Bolton to commemorate her son's fatal jump across the Strid. But as the boy was still alive in 1154 the story goes the way of most folk tales.

Here the Wharfe becomes suddenly narrow, rushing through the dangerous

Strid channel. The sheer power of the water at this point is tremendous. Only a fool would attempt the 'stride', the rocks being usually wet and slippery. People who have fallen in in the past have not re-appeared straight away, finding themselves trapped below underwater ledges and overhangs. So please take great care.

Barden Bridge to Bolton Hall

Follow the path down the western bank of the Wharfe, passing the Cavendish Pavilion, and on downriver to walk up the bank to the roadway. Walk down, past the Cavendish Fountain, to enter via gate the trackway down to the Priory and Hall.

Bolton Hall

Here later ranges are built around the old Priory Gatehouse of the early 14th century. The rib-vaulting archway of the gatehouse is the same as that at Whalley Abbey. The original west entrance is now blocked by a large 16th century fireplace, and in the east entrance is a re-used doorway of c.1370. It has been suggested that this came from the chapter house. The gatehouse is now the dining room of the Hall which is used by the Duke of Devonshire as a shooting lodge.

The Old Rectory

The Old Rectory is built upon the site of the Prior's Infirmary as a school house and paid for by Robert Boyle, the scientist. Part of it is now used as the Parish Office.

The Devonshire Arms

Here you are welcomed by open log fires in surroundings furnished with some individuality using antiques and portraits from Chatsworth, the home of the Duke and Duchess of Devonshire. Apart from the international cuisine served in the elegant restaurant, bar meals are available at very reasonable prices in the public bar. Moorhouses 'Pendle Witch' brew is served along with other fine ales and beers. A good stopping point after a day's walking over Barden Fell.

By the village shop/Post Office is the magnificent Priory Tithe Barn, sadly it is not open to visitors but worth a view all the same.

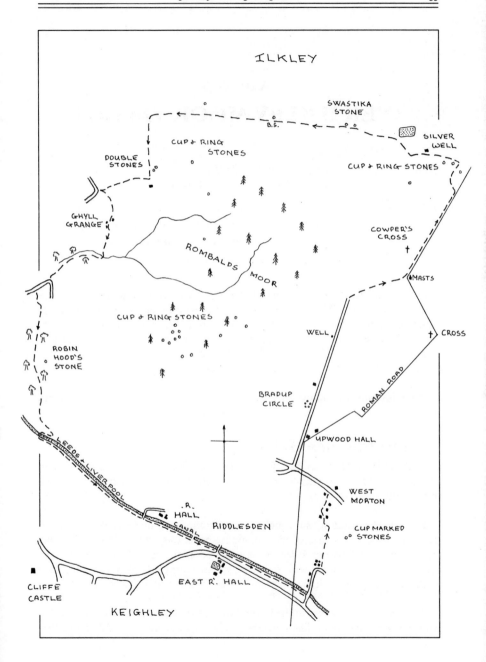

Walk No.7

O'ER ILKLEY MOOR VIA CUT

12 miles, 6 to 7 hours.

MAP: *O.S. sheet SE 04/14*
                    PATHFINDER SERIES.

LUNCH: *Suggest packed lunch, otherwise you could walk*
                    down to find an inn or café in Ilkley by
                    following the moorland track on.

START: *East Riddlesden Hall, Car Park.*

On this walk we follow the line of the Roman road to cross from the Aire Valley to above the Wharfe Valley over that great bulk of wilderness known as Rombalds Moor. We shall study the markings and monuments of the ancient Brigante tribes and wander through the ling-clad moor that once gave sustenance to those peoples. The walk starts and returns via the canal tow path where we shall look at life in the Jacobean past.

To enjoy this area more fully we suggest a visit to Cliffe Castle Museum, Keighley, described at the end of this walk.

East Riddlesden Hall

East Riddlesden Hall was built for the Halifax clothier, James Murgatroyde in the early 1640's. His initials and a date of 1648 appear on a fireplace in the main range.

Entry to the building is through a round-arched porchway flanked by fluted columns. Above is a rose-window of eight spoke, topped-off with battlements and pinnacles. This porch feature is repeated at the rear. Inside the hall we find oak-panelled rooms with richly plastered ceilings displayed in which are collections of pewter, domestic utensils and Yorkshire oak furniture.

The grounds run down to the River Aire and include a formal walled garden and monastic fishpond. The Gift Shop is housed in a former stable range that

EAST RIDDLESDEN HALL BARN

displays a good selection of Yorkshire doorheads, one bearing the date 1642, with the initials I.M.M. & I.S.M. To the right of the Hall porch is the hall of the previous house, and is the oldest part of the building. Attached to this is the ruined range of 1692 of three symmetrical gables. On a side wall is a stone of that date with the initials E.S.M.

Across the pond stands the Great Barn of c.1640, 120 feet long by 40 feet wide, with two big round-arched cart entrances and a sturdy tie-beam roof with king posts. Inside is housed a collection of farm machinery, carts and implements.

The Hall is run by the National Trust, and is open Easter to October. Tel: (0535) 607075. Admission charge for Hall. Great Barn and Car Park free. Well worth a visit.

East Riddlesden Hall to Bradup Circle

Leave by the main gateway and cross the road, then walk up to join the canal tow-path at The Marquis of Granby Inn. Follow tow-path to the right to leave at the next bridge (No.198). Walk up the road, around the corner, then left up Bury Lane Track. Follow the track up, through gates, to enter Dean Hole. Follow the farm lane up to the roadway, left and walk up Street Lane (recalling the nearby Roman road) to go right at crossroads. Walk up Ilkey Road, past Upwood Hall, to go over wall-stile on left at footpath sign. Walk on and over next stile. The stone circle is 40 yards down on the right following the fence.

Brass Castle, Bradup Stone Circle

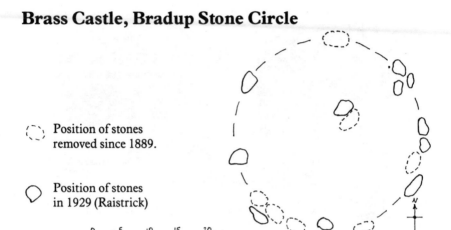

○ Position of stones
   removed since 1889.

○ Position of stones
   in 1929 (Raistrick)

0   5   10   15   20
                        feet

Sited on the rough pasture called "Brass Castle", south west of Bradup Bridge, is a stone circle of c.30 feet diameter. Since 1889 several stones have been removed to repair Bradup Bridge, a deplorable act of vandalism.

There are slight traces of a bank, but the most noticeable feature is the large size of the stones, being Millstone Grit from the nearby escarpment, of which the circle has been constructed. In 1929, Dr. Arthur Raistrick noted some traces of a double circle.

We do not know for sure what function lesser stone circles, like the one at Bradup, performed. Some bear traces of sepulchral monuments, but these appear to be of a later date, and added to an extant monument. With such circles we can dismiss any astronomical possibilities and look instead at the social and economic reasons for their construction.

A wide range of ritual and social activities could have occurred within them which would have left little if any trace: a place for burning bodies before urn burial under mounds etc.; Religious temple site; a market providing for social, economic and genetic interchanges; or the foundations of some building.

What is known is that such circles occupy positions close to the centre of activity in areas of preferred occupation, and their location close to routeways may be associated with the movement of peoples between various sectors in a large resource territory.

Brass Castle
to Cowper's Cross

Return to the roadway and follow it on, past Bradup Farm, and up (notice the old well on the left dated THXS 1853) to go through gate below T.V. mast, and on along the track to Cowper's Cross.

Rombalds Moor

Rombalds Moor takes its name from an ancient trade route that has its origins in the Bronze Age. 'Rombalds Way' starts at the mouth of the Ribble and makes its way on up the valley and through the Aire gap along the Wharfe ridges, across the vale of York by one of the morainic gravel stretches at York or Escrick to the Wolds and the coast.

Along its length it is distinguished by Bronze Age sites, finds and objects, and topographical landmarks. In later Viking times it formed the major route between Dublin and Denmark, via Jorvic (York).

Rombalds Moor is a hive of early settlement. There are five stone circles on the moor, numerous rock carvings, a number of cairns and a network of prehistoric cultivation sites. Radio-carbon determinations indicate that the area was being used for burial intermittently over a period of at least five hundred years — where the builders of such monuments and burial sites lived has not yet been established. Further fieldwork and aerial photography is needed for us to build up a picture of life on Rombalds Moor in relation to the surrounding areas.

The Roman road between the fort at Ilkley (OLICANA?) and the Manchester fort (MAMUCIUM) can be made out making its way over the moor. Its course is recalled in such names as Street Lane, Morton. We follow part of its length between Whetstone Gate and Spicey Gill, by way of Cowper's Cross.

Cowper's Cross is one of two crosses sited on the moor. Carved into the cross stones are the initials ILB IM and the date 1883. Below this point Ilkley is laid out before us, while over to the north west the 'eggs' of the United States spying station dominate the skyline. To the north-west we have a fine view over the southern Yorkshire Dales.

Cowper's Cross to the Swastika Stone

Follow the track down to the tarmac surface. Here follow the track on the left on to Silver Well Cottage. Follow path on to go through wall-gate by shed. Follow the path on through the ferns to join a lower pathway and on to go through wide gap in wall. Follow the path on to the railed-off Swastika Stone.

The Swastika Stone

The Swastika Stone stands behind a natural rock shelf on the summit of Woodhouse Crag, below which the land moves away in a theatre setting. The design on the Swastika Stone on Addingham High Moor resembles designs from Iron Age contexts, but here it is in an area dominated by cup marked and cup and ring marked stones associated, in general, with food vessel cultures.

The carved stones of Rombalds Moor remain an enigma as both their date and function are unclear. They are usually attributed to the Bronze Age as they occur near known Bronze Age remains such as cairns and stone circles.

Nineteenth century antiquarians thought that they were containers for libations offered up in ritual ceremonies. Others thought that they may have been used as primitive maps depicting territorial divisions or were possibly the actual boundary markers of these territories.

It was when first doing the groundwork for this walk that I first came across the Swastika Stone. Having followed the Aire down from Skipton to Keighley, then circumnavigated the whole of the moor, I had gained a good impression of the near landscape in relation to the surrounding areas.

What first struck me when looking at the design on the stone within its position and setting, was a map of the Aire and Wharfe Valleys with Rombalds Moor as the centre of the Swastika:

I took the western arms to represent the Aire Valley and the eastern arms the Wharfe Valley. The S-tail I thought could be a representation of the Brigantian capital of Aldborough (ISVRIVM). The cup-marks within the Swastika,

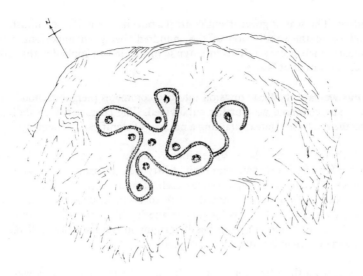

those on the ends of the arms, I took to represent Hill Forts, and the four near to the centre I took to be the caputs of tribal settlements. A possible map of central Brigantia.

The re-occurring pattern-of-five theme within the design is most significant. In Celtic Ireland Tara was the symbolic centre of the island, the kingdom of Midhe (the middle) was fabricated to fit this notion of sovereignty, although its actual existence remains unconfirmed.

This division is called the 'Coiced', "the Fifth Part", although only the four divisions of Ulad (Ulster), Connacht (Connaught), Laigen (Leinster) and Mumu (Munster) are really definable. The fifth was a symbolic, an underlying mythical idea to the early Indo-European peoples.

The Vedas (ancient sacred books of the Hindus, originally brought to India by the Aryans. The Vedas were composed over a long period, probably c.1500-1200 B.C.) contain frequent references to the earth being divided into five parts. Neodruidism of 14th century Wales laid great emphasis on there being five elements rather than the more traditional four.

In political terms, the divisions within a Celtic cantrev are based on the fifth: among the British, as among other Indo-European peoples, the primary political unit, one ruled by a petty king, was often no larger than a mediaeval hundred. The seat of government/court (Caput) in any unit of administration would be in the subdivision of the 'hundred' being an important natural boundary, such as a river. This toponymic principle was applied within all the ancient hundreds of Wales.

Thus we have the basic division into two commotes (neighbourhoods)/land units. The commote was further subdivided. The characteristic subdivision being the multiple estate containing a number of significant settlements.

In the relatively late Venedotian 'model' there were in every Cantrev/Hundred two commotes each of fifty vills/townships. The latter were grouped into twelve multiple estates each of four vills. The four vills that remained, two from each commote, were royal units, demesne and summer pasture (waste), dependant/belonging to the 'fifth' — the royal caput. This form of territorial Organisation has its origins in the Late Bronze/Iron Age, and was a dominant feature within Brigantia.

It is also worth noting that characteristic of the multiple estates was a hill fort near to the central and sub caputs, and, in post Roman times, the most important churches of all, and certainly those which developed into diocesan seats, were located at the administrative cores of the hundreds.

Cup and Ring Marked Rocks

Many authors have been drawn to the question of the meaning of the many marked boulders on the moor. Most have fallen into the trap of building a complex theory upon supposition.

If the reader seeks in this volume another universal theory to explain the mystery of the rock markings — they will be disappointed. The only honest approach to the markings is to lay before the reader observations taken from fact from which the true depth of the mystery can be judged.

A comprehensive field study of the cup and ring stones of the moor has been published by the Yorkshire Archaeological Service. From that survey a few broad conclusions are possible.

The marked stones fall into three main types: cup and ring marked; cup marked only; and more complex designs. The marked boulders tend to be found in clusters on the flanks of the moor — both in Airedale and Wharfedale. Cup and ring marked stones are found in other parts of the British Isles — but Ilkley represents a unique concentration of carvings. It is clear that the stones were cut over a comparatively long period of time — and unfortunately some stones have been recut in modern times. Certain glacial markings may have been interpreted as the hand of man.

The reader cannot avoid asking the question as to what these markings mean, but to ask this question is proof that the reader has a fundamental misunderstanding of the nature of the markings.

Our modern eyes are contaminated by literacy, we look for patterns of words in the stones — names, dates, events and concepts. These markings are the product of a pre-literate society — so could a path to the understanding be found by a comparative study of a modern primitive society?

However, the first stage of colonisation is always cultural genocide. The ways of the past — of the kin group and tribe and local god — are soon replaced by the worst of Western culture and the old ways are lost forever. For if we as a Western Christian society cannot respect or understand the ways of the Amazonian Indians, what hope have we to fathom the mind of man living a thousand years before Christ?

We can be sure however that the stones themselves were sacred in ancient times. The kings of the Picts, the most ancient people we can identify by name in these Isles, were proclaimed upon a stone. This Stone of Scone is now incorporated into the English Coronation Throne in Westminster Abbey. At Hexham and Beverly the thrones of the Anglo-Saxon bishoplords exist cut from a single stone.

In the late 16th century Hugh O'Neill returned from the court of Queen Elizabeth the First to rule his father's kingdom of Tyrone and Tyrconnell. O'Neill returned to Ireland educated as a Renaissance statesman to rule the last Iron Age tribal state in that country.

From the streets of London he came to the windy hillside of Tullaghoge, the inauguration place of the O'Neill kings. In a place much like Ilkley Moor O'Neill, who claimed descent from the legendary Niall of the Nine Hostages, took his seat among the ferns surrounding the king's stone.

Throughout history and throughout the world ancient places of assembly are often signified by stones or physical features — unchanging in a changing world. The significance of certain stones being stressed by the marking of the stone. Sacred marked stones can indeed be found worldwide, from Ilkley Moor to Ayers Rock.

The Swastika Stone to Ghyll Grange

Follow the path on along the ridge, over wall-stile and on to go over next wall-stile. Walk on over Pipers Crag to go over two wall-stiles (notice the Boundary Stone at the second stile — I / M ILB 1893). Follow the path on to go over five stiles and on to the cairn-marked cross junction of paths on Black Hill. Take the left-hand path and walk on to go over wall-stile.

Follow the path directly on down the moor to go through a fence-gate below the wind-eroded formation of Double Stones. Walk on to meet the farm lane and follow it to the right, through gateway and on down to next gateway. Turn around and follow right-hand wall on, through gateway and on down the track to follow driveway down to Ghyll Grange Farm.

Ghyll Grange

Before the Dissolution the Canons of Bolton Priory had a grange farm here (they also had fish ponds at East Riddlesden Hall). The Augustinian Canons of Bolton held the whole manor of Bolton in Wharfedale, the manor of Malham East and much of mid Airedale around and south of Skipton.

From these vast estates they traded extensively in wool, mined lead and did a little iron making, bred horses and ran many farms. There was constant traffic between grange and abbey and the outlying farms. Wool, cheese, grain, building materials and other produce of the granges was carried to the abbey, and ale and food were sent out to the granges.

Thus the granges became a regular feature of the Pennine dales. The grange generally had a chapel for the tenants to hear mass. This and the refectory were in the charge of a priest-monk, and staffed by a group of conversi under supervision from the Priory.

The grange workers cleared vast areas of upland of scrub and established upland farms, thus greatly improving the quality of upland pasture. Their flocks were the ancestors of some of the present dale breeds of sheep.

Life on the monastic estates was not always an idyll. Many resented the way whole tracts of country had been taken from them, in particular the loss of the wild uplands, their former hunting grounds.

At the same time many of the Abbey officials became hard and greedy landlords, not hesitating to deal with tenants in ways quite contrary to the established customs of the manor. In an age before Banks monasteries were often entrusted with deeds and other valuables for safe keeping, and it was not uncommon for the abbots and priors to refuse to return these goods.

Such was the power of the monastic barons. From good intent to pious hypocrisy is but a short step.

Ghyll Grange to Riddlesden

Go through the small gate opposite the garden gate of Ghyll Grange farm cottage. Walk around the farm building and on to go through gates on the right. Follow track down to go through gateway. Walk down the field to go over footbridge, located under the pipeline. Follow the path to the right to go through gateway and on following right-hand fence to go over fence-stile (below is one of a number of waterfalls on Holden Beck).

Walk down, across minor brook and up and on, following edge of wood, to go down bridleway and on to go over stile by gate onto roadway. Walk down the road to go through gate on left at footpath sign. Follow right-hand wall on to enter wood via stile. Follow the path into the wood then after a short way follow the left-hand path up and continue on to leave the wood by a wall-stile up on the left.

Follow right-hand path down to go over stile by gate onto Golf Course. Follow right-hand wall on, then the yellow-staked pathway down to join a gravel trackway and on down, past the club house to go down the trackway on the right and onto the canal tow-path. Follow the tow-path on to the Marquis of Granby Inn, then walk back down the road to East Riddlesden Hall.

West Riddlesden Hall stands in private grounds and you must ask permission before viewing or taking photographs. If you wish to visit then go by way of the first bridge, on returning to the canal from the golf course, and follow the lane around to the right to the Hall and barn.

West Riddlesden Hall

West Riddlesden Hall stands on Scott Lane. The fine facade is of three equal gables with upper oval windows, dated 1687. Mullioned and transomed windows dominate and the deeply moulded doorframe is typical William and Mary.

Nearby stands the 17th century L-shaped barn of five bays with a two bay, two storeyed domestic accommodation to the east. Built at right-angles to the western end is a cow house with loft over. The barn has a waggon entrance to the south opposite a much smaller door to the north. The foundations of a horse-gin occupy the centre of the yard in front of the barn.

Whilst in the Keighley district I would strongly suggest a visit to Cliffe Castle Museum.

Cliffe Castle Museum & Art Gallery

Cliffe Castle was originally the mansion of the worsted manufacturer, Henry Butterfield. Work on this hideous copious pile was begun in 1878 by the architect, George Smith of Bradford. Opulent, yes, but the suite of rooms, with their elaborate French decor and furnishings are a saving grace.

Today's museum contains galleries on local geology that fully explain the underlying landscape of the region. Local wildlife and history exhibits are on view, and a splendid display of minerals and crystals, explaining their structure and formation is not to be missed.

My only comment is that I think that a great deal more could have been done on the History and social and economic development of the area. However, this does not detract from the whole.

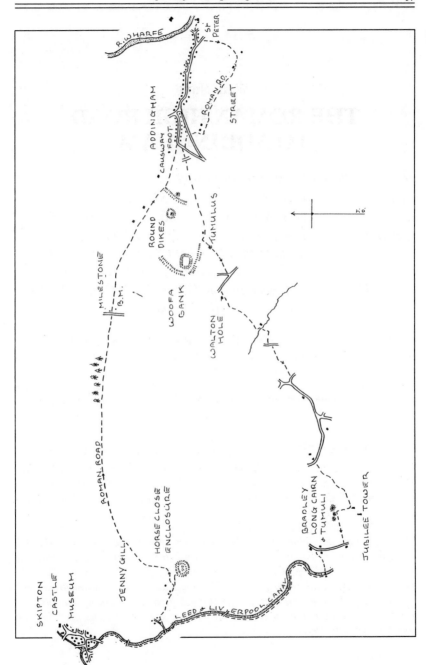

Walk No.8

THE ROMAN HIGH ROAD
TO ADDINGHAM

18 miles, allow 9 hours with lunch stop.

MAPS: *O.S. PATHFINDER SERIES*
                  Nos: SD 84/94 & 85/95. SE 04/14 & 05/15.

GRADE: *Easy, but give yourself a good 9 hours;*
                  Skipton to Addingham 3 hours; lunch 1 hour;
                  Addingham to Skipton, via Bradley 5 hours.

LUNCH: *Addingham: The Sailor Hotel; Craven Heifer;*
                  The Swan — all V.Good.

On this walk we tread in the footfalls of the Roman Legions upon their upland highway between Skipton and Ilkley (OLICANA) gaining magnificent views over the Celtic Cantrevs of Cravenshire, Borgescire and Elmet. Three major Celtic settlements are visited, each standing sentinel above the Brigantian coast-to-coast trade route of Rombalds Way. So without further ado let us return in time to climb the hills of the Welsh Pennines.

Skipton Bus Station to Jenny Gill, Roman Road

Walk out of the Bus Station, right, and on to join the canal tow-path at the Bridge. Follow the tow-path on to leave by bridge No. 180. Walk over the bridge and follow the lane on the right up and round to Lower Caleb's Barn Cottages.

Continue on past Horse Close Farm and on up the trackway to go through fieldgate at corner. Follow track on and round (the other track leads across the ravine and up to Horse Close Enclosure) to the left and on up to follow the wall to the right and on to trackway. Follow track on to go through gateway and on up following wall round to go through gateway. Walk up the hill on a right diagonal, over and on to pass through gateway (fine views over Skipton and Craven from here).

Follow track directly on to go through gateway (there should be a stile down on the left where walls meet). Walk down to wall and follow it on to the Roman Road trackway at Jenny Gill via gate.

Horse Close Enclosure, SD 997505

An excavation conducted by Alan Aberg on a circular stone walled enclosure at Horse Close Farm, Skipton, revealed two hut sites. The larger hut was seen to be oval shape, later converted into a round house, of 26 feet in diameter.

The structure was of timber and in places a 9 inch groove was cut into the bedrock of millstone grit, holding the posts for the walls. There were four 9 inch posts in the centre of the hut circle, being those that held up the roof structure.

The pottery and glass bead found on the site were assigned a pre-Roman Iron Age date, though a Romano-British bronze dress fastening (fibula) was found in the top soil. The other hut was seen to have a sub-rectangular form.

During the work, the major portion of a saddle quern was found in a field wall above Horse Close Hill. And nearby, in the middle of the field alongside Great Wood Laithe (SD 99625055) was noted an outcrop of rock which had almost been levelled with the adjacent field surface by the dumping of boulders from the surrounding ploughland.

On top of the outcrop, that rises to a dome-shaped projection, were found simple cup markings. These average 2 inches in diameter and total 17 in number. The whole surface of the stone is much weathered and good lighting conditions may reveal more details.

Elslack-Ilkley Roman Road

This is by far the longest, most visible and maintained section of Roman Road that can be viewed between the Roman forts of Ribchester (BREMETEN-NACUM), Elslack and Ilkley (OLICANA ?). Being enclosed by 18th century field walls for the major part of its length, one gains a good perspective as to the original width of this military highway — notice the ditch sections at the side also.

Evidence as to the position of Roman roads can often be provided by place-name and field name material. The Old English 'streat' and the Old French 'caucie' in their modern forms 'street, straight, strait' and 'causeway, causey, carsie' can provide such evidence. On the section of Roman road we pass along today we find 'Causeway Foot Farm' and 'Street Farm' standing aside this ancient highway.

We are here following in the footfalls of the Roman Legions, but we are not travelling through the landscape of Roman Imperial Britain. The Imperial period landscape was characterised by large tracts of dense woodland between clearings — excellent territory for guerrilla warfare. The Romans cut the Pennine uplands into blocks with their military roads.

Each side of the road was cleared of cover for about 100 metres (the effective range of the short bow). This method has continued to be used to counter guerrilla tactics into modern times. In Vietnam and in Zimbabwe military roads with free fire zones up to half a mile wide were driven through the guerrilla bush zones.

Except for the main Roman trunk roads it is clear that by the 7th century most Roman roads had fallen into disuse and disrepair.

Bede describes how Bishop Cuthbert and his companions came across a stretch of Roman road in good repair. His younger companions requested and were granted permission to race their horses upon the section of road. This incident shows that a section of Roman road in good order in the 7th century was exceptional in the north of England.

Our present route typifies the force which made most Roman roads redundant. Routes had been laid out by military engineers, who with an eye for ambush took this high route between Skipton (Airedale) and Addingham (Wharfedale) which traverses the flank of the moor inviting ambush only from the higher ground which would have been cleared and controlled.

The modern route between these towns avoids the inclines of that taken by the Roman road and therefore superseded the military road.

Jenny Gill to Addingham

Follow the Roman road up and on, across the Draughton road (notice the old milestone here and the boundary stone by the next section of Roman road, marked with the landowner's initials, J.C.), and on over Addingham Low Moor, past Causeway Foot and on down to the main road (notice the house on the left dated 1797 with the initials J.E.). Right, and walk down the road into the village of Addingham.

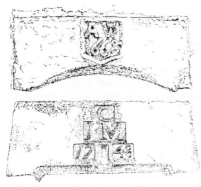

Addingham

Addingham (Odingeham in 1086) is first recorded in the 11th century by the Durham monk, Symeon. He informs us how the Danes invading the north of England, captured York in 867, and how the Archbishop Wulfhere was compelled to flee for his safety and found refuge at 'Hatyngham' in 'Hwervedale' (Wharfedale).

Many houses in the village date from the 17th and 18th century. A good doorhead is to be found at the village library, dated 1668 with the initials A.W. Representing the 18th century is a house opposite the Sailor Hotel, dated 1790 with the initials I.C.M., and another, further down the road, is dated 1748 with the same initials.

To St. Peter's Church

Walk on through the village to turn left down Church Street on into North Street. Follow footpath sign opposite, over the little bridge and on into the churchyard.

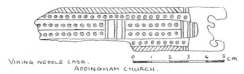

VIKING NEEDLE CASE.
ADDINGHAM CHURCH.

St. Peter, Addingham

This riverside church is reached by one or other narrow one-arched bridges that date from the 17th or 18th century. Most of the work is uninspiring and dates from 1757. But close inspection reveals a Perpendicular church of c.1475: the north aisle with low three-light windows, straight-headed with round-arched lights; the arcade of three bays with octagonal piers; and the nave roof with tie-beams and king-posts. This work was done when a Vavasour (lords of the manor) was both squire and rector.

At the rear of the church can be found the bottom section of an early 11th century cross. This was found in 1948 and is of course sandstone. The face displays two small figures below a cross in a circle with a pair of 'chains' above, the sides being decorated with interlacing cords within panels. The base of this cross was found to the east of the church (SE 086496) and displays swirl decoration on its face. It is now sited near a table grave south-east of the church.

On display inside the church is a possible Scandinavian comb or needle case. The combination of dot and circle ornament and the border decoration tend to place it in the Viking period. The case was found east of the church in 1972 in the sealing level of an Iron Age ditch which surrounded the land on which the church was built.

Excavations in the grounds of Addingham Rectory, to the east of the church, have produced Scandinavian material from the Late Anglo-Saxon period. This was the site of the pre-Conquest thegn's hall. Such a place would have been well established here when Archbishop Wulfhere sought refuge here from the Danes in 867.

Addingham may have formed part of the Archbishop of York's Otley estate in the 7th century, and was listed amongst his alienated estates by Archbishop Oswald in the late 10th century. It was never recovered by the archbishop and remained in lay hands, as Gamalbarn held the whole of Addingham in 1066. By 1086 one carucate was held by the king and two by Gislebert Tison.

The Domesday Survey refers to 'Edidham/Ediham' as a manor and 'Odingeham/Odingehen' as a soke of Bolton — both are traditionally identified as Addingham. Although the tenancy-in-chief remained split between the honour of Skipton and the Percy Fee, William le Vavasour held both moieties of the vill as mesne in 1166.

In our introduction we mentioned the visit of St. Cadrow to Addingham and the Archbishops' palace here (rectory). We now put this visit into context:

On a spring evening around 950 A.D. Saint Cadrow came by way of Addingham. A few hours before Cadrow's party arrived an outrider would have told the Archbishop's reeve to be prepared to receive Abbot Cadrow — the leading Pictish churchman of his age.

In the late afternoon the horns of the party would have been heard in the distance. The horns were blown to signify that this was not a warband. As the party came within sight a young priest led the way and though on horseback he carried a rude wooden cross on high. Behind came the bodyguard provided by the King of Strathclyde — maybe a dozen warriors dressed in the dark brownish plaid of the lowlands.

The plaid — an uncut length of eight or so metres was wrapped around the waist and thrown over the shoulder — the crude ancestor of modern Highland dress. Some hold that the mediaeval kilt owed its origins to the Caledonian chiefs wearing a Toga-like garment in imitation of Roman aristocracy. The men of Strathclyde are said to have fought naked with lance, sword and bow.

The bodyguard of Catrow's party rode stocky lowland ponies. In normal times a holy monk would disdain riding, but in these times of unrest the best security policy was to move quickly through the disputed lands of the west and central Pennines.

Cadrow would have first noted the smoke of cooking fires at a few miles distant from Addingham, then the settlement itself would have come into view.

The Archbishop's enclosure probably dated back to a Celtic foundation built like the Whalley Celtic monastery of Paegnalaech within a vallum by a river crossing. On the site of the present parish church stood the chapel of the estate, probably built of stone. In the graveyard would have stood a number of stone crosses — over twelve feet tall and painted as bright as a pagan totem.

Outside the vallum would have been grouped twenty or so peasants' huts. Within the vallum the main building was a hall of over 30 metres in length. Around the hall stood other huts used for storage, barns, byers and cooking. Except for the church all would have been constructed of wood, earth and thatch.

In early spring, in the centre of the great hall, a fire would burn by day and night. Privacy was an unknown concept in this society. Having prayed together the party would retire to the hall for a meal of bread or gruel with meats and ales taken on low tressels and benches. As darkness fell monk and warrior, master and slave, kin and stranger would sleep in the common hall amid the straw and general debris of the floor.

This was the Archbishop's palace at Addingham.

St. Peter's to Parson's Lane Tumulus

Walk back to North Street and along Church Street to the main road, left, and cross the road to turn right into the cricket ground. Walk on towards the pavilion to go over a fence-stile over on the left. Follow the path up to go through kissing-gate and on through gates over the line of the old railway. Follow left-hand fence up and around to the right to go over stile in corner at Street Farm (we are now back on the line of the Roman road).

Follow line of wall on past the corner and on to go through gateway. Follow track on, over stile and on to go over new roadway and on to follow right-hand wall/hedgerow to go through gateway over on the left. Follow left-hand hedgerow on, over stile and through three gates to go over ford.

Follow right-hand fence down, through gate to footbridge (DO NOT GO OVER). Left, and cross the stream to follow path up to go through gate. Follow path to roadway and pass through gate opposite to follow far wall up to go through kissing-gate. Right, then first left on up over the new road and on up Parson's Lane to go through gate on left at the top of the trackway. Follow the walled droveway on, around the corner to the bowl-barrow tumulus.

Round Dykes and Woofa Bank

Upon Addingham Low Moor two probably non-defensive oval earthworks are to be found, being known as Round Dykes and Woofa Bank. Both sites are overlooked by the surrounding steep terrain. The earthworks are bounded by a linear bank to which they are thought not to be related, though according to the Ordnance Survey, the earthwork at Woofa Bank could be a boundary earthwork contemporary with this enclosure. The interior of Woofa Bank enclosure is above the surrounding surface, as at Catstones Ring enclosure above Bingley (SE 06803808).

A limited survey of parts of Round Dykes defined nine hut circles or parts of circles and possible hearth sites. Both earthworks require a full further survey for the ground evidence to be evident. Both sites are ascribed to the Iron Age, but the Tumuli at Round Dykes are seen to be Bronze Age in origin. The tumulus on the trackway below Woofa Bank is a typical ring/bowl barrow, again ascribed to the Bronze Age.

Each of these barrows will, if not already robbed, contain at least one urn burial. It is from the study of urn decoration and form, plus carbon dating, that a date can be put on the erection of such structures.

A bronze spearhead has been the only tangible find in the area, this was discovered at the Addingham end of Parson's Lane.

Woofa Bank to Walton Hole

Follow the droveway on to Bank Lane, left, then right to go down Cringles Lane to take the first trackway on the left down to Walton Hole farm.

Walton Hole

At the time of writing (October 1989) the farmstead at Walton Hole stands derelict and forlorn, and looks like having done so for the last few years.

The doorhead bears a date of 1719 with the initials H.F.A. All the windows have chamfered mullions and inside can be seen a large open hearth with side-ovens.

Bread was baked in the side-oven. Oven wood or hot peat was placed in the oven until it reached the required temperature when the embers were brushed out, the loaves were introduced and the door sealed up. When the oven cooled down the bread was baked.

At that time wheat bread was rare in the Pennines, oats being the principal cereal grown. The oats were ground at the local mill to be made into havercake on the kitchen backstone, being a metal plate or thin stone slab placed over a separate fireplace. The oatmeal was mixed with water and the mixture then poured on to a wooden board covered with muslin, from which it was transferred to the backstone. After a few moments the havercake was turned by means of a wooden 'spittle'. Then it was hung over the 'bread-creel' to dry. Havercake was a staple food throughout the Pennine region until the mid-19th century.

The place-name Walton Hole contains the element 'Walh' and could possibly have its origins in the post-Roman British period, meaning 'of the British (Welsh/Celtic)', though the name itself is not recorded until the tithe award of 1858 There is evidence of ridge and furrow, a hollow-way and earthworks likely to go back to the Middle Ages.

Walton Hole to Low Bradley Moor

Follow the track down to go over footbridge. Follow the path on up, bearing to the left to go through small gate in fence over on left. Follow right-hand fence on to go over wall-stile near corner of walls by gates. Follow left-hand wall/fence on to go through gateway. Walk down track to farm entrance, right and down to go over footbridge, up and over stile. Follow right-hand fence on to go through gate on right at corner.

Walk on to go over wall-stile at corner of building. Follow the wall around to the right and on along the edge of the field to go over wall-stile onto lane. Left, and walk up to go over wall-stile on right. Follow right-hand fence on to go over wall-stile and on, following left-hand hedge to go through hedge-gate (this is often overgrown, if so follow hedge to the right and step over the low fence). Follow right-hand hedgerow on, through gateway and on to the roadway via stile by gate. Walk up the road to the junction, left, and walk on, right at next junction then on, around and up to the triangulation point.

Walk on a few yards or so to go over wall-stile on left. Walk on, veering to the right, to go over wall-stile. Cross the field on a left diagonal to go over wall-stile. Follow path on to go over wall-stile down on the right. Cross the moor to the giant cairn. From here walk up to the far wall. Look over the wall, the piles of stones are the remains of the barrows.

The Bradley Barrows

On Black Hill, Bradley Low Moor, we find three early burial places: a Neolithic long barrow, a large circular stone barrow, and a smaller late Bronze Age circular bank barrow. The latter two are much disturbed, possibly having been robbed at some time. The long barrow was excavated in the 1930's and

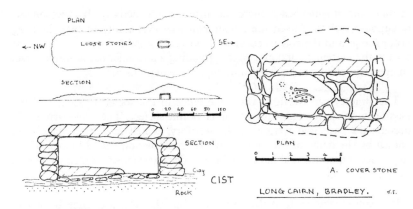

LONG CAIRN, BRADLEY.

was found to be a Neolithic long cairn with a later round cairn imposed upon it. The mound is c.250 feet long and rises to a present maximum height of 8 feet at its eastern end.

The excavation revealed a stone cist, 6½ feet long and 3 feet wide, some 60 feet from the eastern end of the barrow. The cist was formed by four stone slabs set on end with a fifth forming a 'capstone'. A sixth slab lay on the floor and this covered a deposit of unburnt but smashed human bones. Cremated bones were also found in the cist. The mound contained a number of standing stones, but none of these formed a second cist. The barrow may represent a degenerate example of a megalithic chambered tomb.

The Bradley long barrow is the only one of its type in west Yorkshire, its nearest 'relative' standing on Anglezarke Moor above Chorley in Lancashire (see 'HISTORIC WALKS AROUND THE WEST PENNINE MOORS' by John Dixon and Jaana Järvinen. Carnegie Press, Preston. 1988).

This megalithic structure represents the product of a high point in Late Neolithic society in this part of the Pennines.

The building of such a large monument would have consumed an appreciable share of the community's time, energy and effort. Its construction and use would to some extent have performed a communal function, although it was probably directed by and for a small elite.

The building of the tomb would take twenty or so able-bodied persons over thirty days. Such an investment of labour would have to be made over a period of time, and at times when there was little farming activity. It is reasonable to suppose that they used the labour potential availability of neighbouring groups to join in the construction work. Given a suitable incentive — a great feast with amusement and exchanges providing a forum for social intercourse, co-operative effort can work to build impressive monuments.

The Bradley cairn reflects the importance of the social occasion and the passionate concern for group status in Neolithic society. The long cairn would become the principal feature of the territory, which may itself have been known by the name of the monument. Its construction would be one of the steps such a group would have to take in order to establish its identity within the regional clan.

It is conceivable that, in the Atlantic facade that this area then belonged, swidden agriculture was practised — the village would remain in one place for a decade or so and then, as the land nearby became exhausted, move on to new land in the same territory.

The tomb would provide a territorial foci point for that family group, an enduring symbol of the continuity of their occupation of that land. Each group would consist of around thirty persons — a single farming family, belonging to a larger folk/clan spread throughout the region, each group holding one territory.

Black Hill to Skipton

Follow the wall down to the roadway, right, and walk on over the brow, and down to go over stile by gate on left. Follow the track down, through gateway and on down to go through bottom gate on left and on down to the canal tow-path via the swing-bridge. Follow the tow-path northwards to the centre of Skipton.

Bronze Age Mound, Skipton

An accessory cup, with cord impressions, was found beneath the pavement in Keighley Road, Skipton. It is presumably from a destroyed burial mound. The cup can be viewed in the Craven Museum, Skipton (No. 59: Classified as early Bronze Age). It is possible that this barrow is related to the Horse Close enclosure site, and points to a nearby lower settlement.

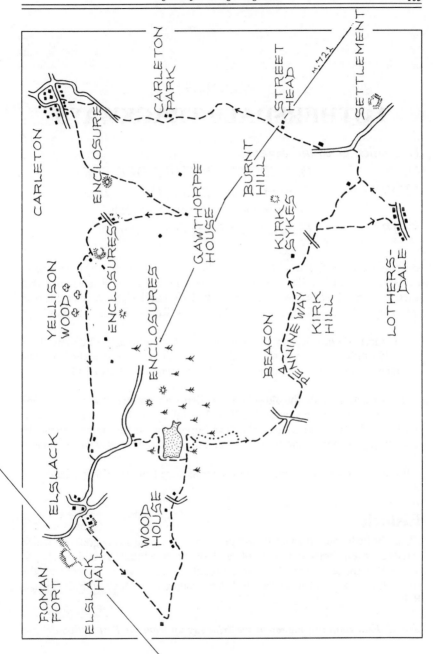

Walk No.9

LOTHERSDALE TRACKWAYS

11½ miles. Good hill walking.

MAP: *O.S. SD 84/94 PATHFINDER SERIES.*

LUNCH: *Tempest Arms, Elslack; Hare & Hounds,*
      Lothersdale; The Swan, Carleton.

START: *Lothersdale, Elslack or Carleton.*

On this walk we follow a number of old trackways through this moorland landscape of Craven. The oldest track to be followed is the Roman road that once formed a link between the fort at Elslack and Keighley, referred to as 'Margary 721' (listed in Ivan Donald Margary's 'Roman Roads in Britain').

The most recent trackway that we shall wander along is the Pennine Way. This 250 mile walk along the "backbone" of England, established by The Ramblers' Association, was officially declared open on 24th April 1965.

Other tracks include the old salters way that went through the area between Colne and Skipton, and those that link the high moor with village known as herdways. All these tracks have played an important role throughout history in developing the local economy and forming the landscape as we know it today.

From the writer's view only, I start the walk here from the tiny settlement of Elslack.

Elslack

Elslack is little more than a few cottages huddled around a tiny green on which stands a curious horse mounting block. I am informed that the wedged-shaped stones that make up the block were brought from Haworth. A barn on the right of the entry lane to Elslack Hall has a datestone of 1672 with the initials R.B.

Elslack Hall stands at the top of the driveway up from the Post Office.

Elslack Hall

In 1270 the manor of Elslack was granted to Geoffry de Altaripa, who some time later built his Hall here. In 1318, during the reign of Edward II, Godfrey de Altaripa was granted a licence to 'kernel and embattle' Elslack Hall. This was only four years after the Battle of Bannockburn, when previously Craven had been devastated by Scottish raids, a time when invasion fears were still very real.

Fragments from the mediaeval early 14th century Hall can still be discerned. The mediaeval part of the hall has a slightly projecting former staircase-well and some small lancet windows. The moat also belongs to this early period. The porch and the eastern section, with six-light windows with arched lights, belong to the 17th century.

The manor descended from the Altaripas to the Radcliffes to the Malhams. The last of the Malhams was Colonel Francis Malham Esq, a Royalist, who died just before the Restoration of the Monarchy.

The field to the west of Elslack Hall holds a number of earthen habitation platforms and a large ditched rectangular earthwork. Look out for these on the path from Elslack to Brown House.

Elslack Hall to Roman Fort

Come down the drive and follow the road to the left to the first farmhouse. Here ask permission to walk up onto the railway to gain access to the fort site via a sign-marked gate.

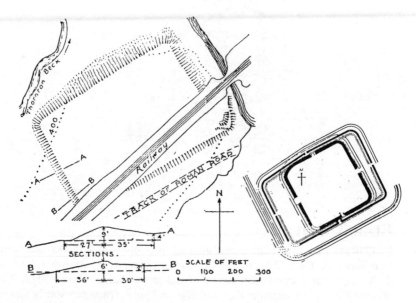

Burwen Castle, Elslack Roman Fort

The earthwork known as Burwen Castle is a large rectangular plateau, some 600 ft. by 400 ft. and covering 5¼ acres, just west of the former Elslack railway station, in the angle formed by Thornton Beck and a tributary. The railway has cut through it in a slanting direction, close to its edge, and has destroyed the south west angle. The slopes on all sides are irregular and it is only their crest which forms such a definitive rectangle. It is only in the west that any remains of ramparts are visible.

The site was excavated in 1908 and 1910 and finds from the site can be seen in the Craven Museum, Skipton. These include: a late Bronze Age palstave, leather boots, horse trappings, an iron linchpin, a Samian bowl, copper coins of Domitian (86 A.D.) and Constantine (31237 A.D.), an upper stone of a rotary quern made of lava and imported from Germany, and an artillery stone for a carroballista found outside the fort.

The reason for the initial establishment of military sites in the old West Riding of Yorkshire seems to have been the control of the Brigantes. Brigantian resistance had its core in the central Pennine areas running southwards from Wharfedale and Craven, where the terrain was well suited to a resistance movement. Each of the prominent dales along which Roman roads ran had a major fort, the Wharfedale region was controlled from Ilkley (OLICANA ?), with smaller forts at Elslack and Long Preston being established to deal with local populations. The Elslack fort was established in the initial conquest phase, along with Ribchester and Ilkley.

The first fortification at Elslack was built during the campaigns of Agricola c.80 A.D., being small in size and having clay ramparts. This was succeeded by a larger stone one. The present remains are of the last large 4th century camp. Some writers hold Elslack to be OLICANA (S. Frere. 'Britania'), but the fort at Ilkley is a more likely candidate.

During 1988 a Geophysical Survey was undertaken upon the Roman fort site at Elslack. This revealed a building at the back of the eastern fort wall, approx. 16m. x 8m. The fort interior showed little evidence of any substantial structures.

Elslack Hall to Pinhaw Beacon

On the right of Elslack Hall farm barn go over a stile at the Earby footpath sign and follow line of wall on to go over corner wall-stile. Follow trackway, through small gate by gate, on to end. Go over the stile by the middle gate and follow right-hand wall, then stream, on to cross the stream by stiles into field. Cross the field to far fence and follow it on to near the stile by Brown House farmyard.

Here go left up the hill to veer left at the lone ash tree crossing the field to go over footbridge and fence stile. Follow line of right-hand fence up the clough to go over fence stile. Follow the path up to go through gateway. Here we leave the 'Pennine Way' to follow the track on, through the next gateway, to Wood House farm. Follow the farm lane, past Park House, to roadway. Pass through the gateway on the right opposite and follow left-hand wall on, past the 18th century Cooper House, to go through gate into wood.

Follow forest track on to where it meets a track coming up from Elslack Reservoir on the left (if you wish to view the two Standrise Enclosures follow the track down and on to Stories House by the roadway to obtain permission to enter the field from Moor Lane on the return leg from Carleton).

From now on the true definitive public right of way is impossible to follow, due to the negligence and 'couldn't-give-a-damn' attitude of the plantation owners. The path that I shall direct you along is the one used by local ramblers to get round this problem.

Continue along the track to the top of the rise to go right, up the pine-lined pathway to veer right by the wall near the top of the wood. Follow wall up and onto the moor via gap in fence. Follow the wall to the right to the edge of the wood. Walk up the moor, veering slightly to the right to the high point of the roadway. Right, and walk on down the road to junction to go left at 'Pennine Way' sign. Follow the trackway on to Pinhaw trig. point.

Pinhaw Beacon

At the highest point above the road that in the 17th century connected Colne to Skipton, via Carleton, stands the ancient beacon of Pinhaw. These 'land lighthouses' have been used since Roman times to guide the traveller through difficult countryside or to warn of some event or danger.

In the early 1800's the Pinhaw fire beacon had six guards appointed to it — two each from Lothersdale, Elslack and Carleton, each pair manning the beacon for a week at a spell, and a hut was provided for the guards to live in.

To the south-west we can observe Bleara Lowe and the Tumulus burial mound. Upon excavation the mound produced several sherds of Bronze Age pottery. These can now be seen in the Craven Museum, Skipton. On the east side of Bleara Lowe is Salt Pye Farm, recalling the ancient Salt Road that ran from the Northwich salterns to Knaresborough, via Manchester, Colne and Skipton. As this road leaves Colne we find the name of Salter Syke Farm, again recalling the old salt road.

A Salt Pie, however, refers to a definite structure. This would have been a sturdily built storehouse, small in size, usually sited near cross-roads or on the edge of a village. From here salt would be stored for later distribution to farmsteads and villages; in this case Earby, Lothersdale and the surrounding farms.

Pinhaw Beacon to Hare & Hounds, Lothersdale

Follow the moorland path on to go over wall-stile above Kirk Sykes farm. Follow the wall down to go over wall-stile onto farm road and walk down to the public roadway. Go over wall-stile opposite and follow left-hand wall down to go over wall-stile by gate. Follow right-hand wall down, over the clough, and on, still following right-hand wall then fence to go over stile by gate on the right. Follow the track down to Lothersdale.

The Hare & Hounds is down on the right.

Lothersdale

The derivation of the place-name Lothersdale is the 'beggars or poor man's allotments (doles)', and is recorded as such in the Norman Survey of 1086 — "In Lodresdene and Carlentone 10 carucates for geld (to be taxed), it formerly belonged to Gamel, now Roger of Poitou has it."

Until recently, Lothersdale contained about forty farmsteads and smallholdings. Open fields around the village were cultivated, the higher lands for pasture. Plough marks, displaying the typical reversed S-shape of ox ploughing, can be made out to the west of the village near Wedding Hall Fold. A few of the later 17th century farmhouses can still be found within the dale, a good example being Woodhead Farm, located on the southern Lothersdale section of the 'Pennine Way'. The doorhead of the porch bears the inscription:

S
Fear you the   P   M   Lest you be cut
Lord God   off with the sword

The initials belong to Peter Scarbrough, and his wife, of Kildwick Grange. His initials and a date of 1673 appear upon a fire mantel inside. Above the doorhead is a stone tablet with the following verse carved upon it:

If thou with sin afflicted be
O then saith Christ come thou to me
I am the way walke thou to me
Embrace the truth abandon sin

Away we must return to dust
There is no thing more sure
Therefore in time let us repent
Gods kingdom to procure

Hugh Deane fecit An Dom 1673

Other houses of note are: Stone Gappe below Four Lane Ends, Knott Farm below White Hill, and Further Surgil Head on the Hawshaw Road.

On Rook Street, with later cottages adjoining, is Stansfield House dated 1752, with the initials of John Slater & Isabel Walker, very typical for the period.

Lothersdale to Babyhouse Lane

Come out of the Hare & Hounds and follow the road to the left, along Rook Street and on up to go first left to enter Bridleway. Follow track up to go through gate onto farm lane. Walk on to go over wall-stile on right. Follow left-hand wall on to go over wall-stile by gate onto Babyhouse Lane.

Four Lane Ends

Babyhouse Lane? No, I do not know where this name comes from. What I do know is that in 1810 it is recorded as Babby House Gate.

Four Lane Ends was in ancient times the site of the Lothersdale gallows and gibbet. Thomas de Altaripa, lord of the manor of Lothersdale, was recorded in 1278 of acting as sheriff, judge and jury over all legal concerns in the district. Criminals who he found guilty, and if their deeds warranted it, would be hanged and later displayed at Four Lane Ends.

All this he did on his own account without having received the Royal sanction. Tradition holds that the last man to be gibboted here was named Singleton and that it was for horse stealing. This was in the early 1800's. The de Altaripa's also had gallows in Carleton.

From our vantage point at the site we can view over on the left Bradley High Moor, in front of us Rombalds Moor, while over on the far right the 'salt & pepper pots' of Lund's Tower and Wainman's Pinnacle compete for the eye.

To the near left is Gib Hill with its chimney. This is part of a lead mining complex that reached its zenith in the last century, when in the early 1800's the Duke of Devonshire brought up miners from Cornwall to extract the ore there.

An explanation of the workings can be gained with a visit to Earby Mines Museum where the story of lead mining in Yorkshire is vividly told. Lothersdale has a long history of mining. Lead, Iron, Barytes and Lime industries have in their time brought much needed employment to the area.

Just down Babyhouse Lane, over on the left, are the earthwork remains of an Iron Age/Romano-British settlement site, the earliest home of man in the area, being a pentagonal ditched earthwork with an entrance on the east and covering just over one acre.

Babyhouse Lane to Street Head

Follow the lane to the left to enter first farm lane on right. Walk on to go over wall-stile on the left. Follow right-hand wall on, through gateway and over two wall-stiles onto Street Head farm trackway.

Street Head

The lane leading up to Street Head farm from the road below is part of the Roman road from Keighley to Elslack (Margary 721). Moor Lane at Standrise is also on the line of this road.

To the west of Street Head is Cross Green. Here a 17th century farmstead and 14½ acres of land are surrounded by rectangular dry ditch ramparts. The ramparts are 1ft. 2in. high and 16ft. wide. The ditch is 27ft. wide, and height from rampart top to ditch bottom is 5ft. The four corners face the cardinal points.

The nature of this earthwork may be similar to that of Bomber Camp near Gisburn.

Street Head to Carleton, The Swan Inn

Cross the field on a right diagonal to go over wall-stile. Follow right-hand wall on (good views over Airedale) to go over wall-stile by old gateway. Follow wall on the left down to go over wall-stile on left.

Follow left-hand wall down (Ingleborough, Pen-y-ghent, Malham and Flasby Fell all now come into view) to go over wall-stile and on across the field to go through gateway onto driveway. Walk directly on to go through gateway opposite.

Follow right-hand wall on for half its length, then head over to the left to go over corner wall-stile. Walk on to go over wall-stile over on left, then follow path to the right to go over stile and on to the roadway. Right, and walk down the road to go over wall-stile on left near bench. Follow left-hand wall down to go over damaged wall-stile. Follow wall down to the right and on at corner to go over fence-stile at new houses. Walk down, across the drive and down the steps to follow path on to roadway at bridge.

Follow the road to the right, past the mill and on to the Swan Inn.

Carleton

The tricephalic stone head pictured here was unearthed some years ago in the garden of 'Gala Stones', Beck View. It is 7½ inches high and of coarse sandstone. The face is much weathered, but the eyes have upper and lower eyelids joined in a continuous oval.

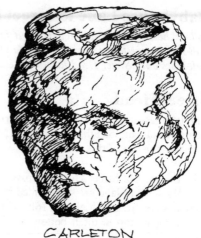

CARLETON
SD. 9749

Where each ear should be there is what may be intended to represent an animal head, the eyes indicated by mere hollows. Only the head on the right side of the main head has a mouth. There is a deep hollow in the crown, surrounded by a rim. This hollow may have been used as a receptical for offerings of a votive nature.

The Swan makes for an attractive and excellent lunch venue, good beer and good home cooking. The village holds little of architectural note, but the houses in Beckside, especially Trappes Hall, are worth viewing.

The Swan, Carleton, to Catlow Gill Enclosure

Walk back to the bridge and on up to go left into The Wend. Follow The Wend trackway on, over bridge and past buildings on up to go through gateway. Follow the track on, through three gateways and on over to the left, following waymarkers on, then down to go over fence-stile. Walk up the banking to the Enclosure.

Catlow Gill Enclosure

Like the other enclosures we pass on this walk the earthwork at Catlow Gill is a native settlement once occupied by the local Brigantian community, whose labour produced the food supplies to support the inhabitants of the Roman forts and towns. The Iron Age way of life still dominated the economy and agriculture, and these sites may pre-date the Roman occupation.

The Catlow Gill enclosure is sited on the middle slope of a hillside above a ravine where two streams meet and this is significant. It covers a large oval area and is surrounded with a ditch and bank.

It is not impossible that lead was mined in the area during the Roman period. We do know that the deposits at Cononly were worked in the post-mediaeval period. Evidence of lead working was found during the excavations at Elslack fort.

Catlow Gill Enclosure to Scarcliff Enclosure

Walk up the hill to go over wall-stile. Walk over to far right corner of field to go through gateway. Follow track on then down to cross the stream and over wall-stile. Walk up the banking on a left diagonal and on to go over wall-stile. Cross the field to go through gateway near farm. Pass through the gate on the right and walk down the field, veering to the left to go through gateway and on down to the left to go through next gateway. Follow left-hand wall down to follow trackway up and on to road. Right, and walk on to go up farm lane on left. Follow the trackway on to Yellison Farm cattle-grid. The Enclosure is up and over on the left and you do need permission of the farmer to view.

Yellison

Only a couple of farmsteads stand around Scarcliff today, Yellison Farm is one of them. But in 1538 Yoleson is recorded as being a village.

Yellison Farm to Elslack

Cross the cattle-grid and walk on to go through gateway. Follow trackway down to go over cattle-grid. Follow left-hand wall on to go through gateway at corner of Yellison Wood. Follow right-hand wall on to go through gate on right. Follow left-hand wall on to go through gate on left. Follow right-hand wall on to go through gate on right. Follow left-hand wall on to go over wall-stile and directly on to go over corner wall-stile. Follow right-hand wall on to go over wall-stile. Walk directly on to go through gate at far right corner of field. Cross the field on a right diagonal to enter farmyard. Follow farm lane on to roadway. Right, and follow the road on to Elslack.

The Tempest Arms is down the road, past the fort site, near the Colne and Broughton road.

Down the road from Elslack, at Broughton in Craven, a Bronze Age barrow was opened in 1675. A large urn was seen to contain a tanged bronze knife, a perforated stone axe-head and a whetstone.

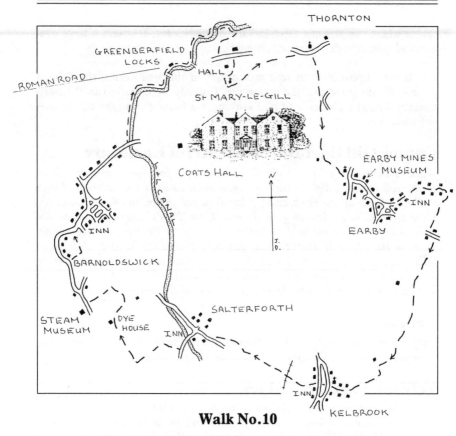

Walk No.10

WEST CRAVEN VILLAGES

9½ miles, 4 to 5 hours, easy walking.

MAP: *O.S. 84/94 PATHFINDER SERIES.*

LUNCH: *Red Lion, Earby; Cross Keys, Barnoldswick;*
              Anchor Inn, Salterforth.

START: *Barnoldswick Outdoor Shop/Tourist Information*
              Centre — 'Old Library'.

PARKING: *Public parking in front of Leo's.*

On this walk we explore three old West Riding villages that have been usurped by Red Rose Lancashire, now administered by Pendle Borough. West

Craven is nestled below the Pennine gritstones, a drumlin landscape of rolling bers (hills) set on a bed of limestone, that has more in common with Thomas Hardy country than the mother mass of Pendle. Here lonely field churches dwell in rural seclusion, wayside cottage gardens are decked in floral profusion, scents from which cling to the air.

The way and pace of life here bears no relation to Pendle's industrial sprawls; here a quieter life ensues, unensnared by the consumerism that has destroyed so many other rural retreats. Truely an exploration of joy and wonder in this now White Rose corner of Lancashire.

BARNOLDSWICK

Barnoldswick in Craven

Sheltered by the great mass of Weets Hill we find the ancient township of Barnoldswick, recorded in Domesday as 'Bernulfeswic' and known affectionately by the locals as 'Barlick'.

The centre of the town still retains the narrow cottage lined streets of its pre-industrial past, and amongst these can be found a number of 17th and early 18th century farmsteads and houses that formed the original village. Good examples being a house of c.1660 in a courtyard of Walmsgate, now partially obscured but complete with its original mullioned windows. Notice too the stone head set in the wall opposite.

Another ancient dwelling stands above the Cross Keys (the oldest inn in the town) at the rear of the Town Hall. Here an old farmhouse has been converted into a number of cottages and the barn has become a drinking club. A doorhead on the south elevation bears the date 1714 with the initials I.E.Y.

The town now boasts a new Town Square, located on Albert Road on the site of the old Co-op buildings. Here can be found the Victorian Jubilee Fountain that once stood near the Commercial Hotel at the Butts before being 'hidden' within Letcliff Park. With its Square, Victorian shops, friendly inns, canal and Park developments and a Tourist Information Centre (located in the old Library along with a very good Outdoor Equipment Centre) Barnoldswick has much to offer the native and visitor alike.

Leo's Car Park to St. Mary-le-Gill

Follow the main road down to go right onto Skipton Road. Follow Skipton Road on to join the canal tow-path at the bridge. Follow the tow-path on, past Greenberfield Locks to go over a bridge onto the opposite tow-path. Walk on around the corner to go over wall-stile on the right at 'Pendle Way' sign. Follow the path up and to the right to go over stile by gate.

Follow track to the left to go over wall-stile by gate onto lane above Rolls Royce factory (you are now standing on the Roman Road that once ran between the forts of Ribchester and Elslack). Cross the main road and walk down the grass verge for a short way to go through small gate opposite Rolls Royce factory entrance. Follow path up, passing Gill Hall, to enter the churchyard.

Gill Hall

I know very little of the origins of Gill Hall, only that in 1727 Ann Heber married Thomas Sawley of Gill Hall and that Gill Hall was regarded as the manor house of the area. Later it was used as a rectory and today it is but a simple farmhouse.

Viewed from the roadway it would pass unnoticed, it is only when you come upon its southern elevation that its ancient nature is perceived. Its upper and lower pairs of five-light mullioned and transomed windows suggest a late 16th century date, as too does the doorhead. The remains of a fireplace and a bricked-up doorway on the east end point to a once much larger structure. All in all very pleasing.

The Gill stands above Greenberfield Locks that raise the Leeds and Liverpool Canal to the summit level 487ft. above sea level. In former times there was a three-rise lock-staircase here but this used so much water that it was replaced by three single locks in 1820. This work caused the canal to be diverted, yet the old route is still clearly visible, including the redundant bridge which was turned into a stable for the barge horses.

Notice, too, the old limekiln that stands above the second lock. The locks have now been developed into a picnic site, and on a warm summer's day it is most relaxing to watch the colourful narrow boats gracefully rise or descend amid the rustic greenery.

To the south of Greenberfield stands the stately eminence of Coats Hall. The Hall is a seven-bay house of c.1700, with cross windows on two floors. The large doorway is flanked by coupled fluted columns with a classical pediment above. Coats was formerly a grange farm of Sawley Abbey. William Drake owned the estate in 1677, and later built the present Coats Hall.

ST MARY-LE-GILL

St. Mary-le-Gill

My heart is always lifted when seeing the simple stepped lancets on the east window of some lonely village church, slender stone reminders of the fate of three on a Friday afternoon at the Place of the Skull, Golgotha. And indeed what a place for quiet reflection this churchyard is amid the willow-herb, brome, wild-thorn and old English rose that play for space among the tangled stones.

The church has a fine Perpendicular bell-tower, bearing a date on the south face of 1524. By the porch an old stone coffin rests, and by the priest's door can be found the churchyard's oldest gravestone, 1609.

Inside the church we are greeted by an array of Jacobean box-pews, and set against the north wall a three-decker pulpit with an octagonal sounding board above. It combines the parish clerk's seat, a lectern and a pulpit. The service would be conducted from the lectern and the responses from the lowest stall. From the highest stall would be preached the sermon. These lofty pulpits became necessary when high bow-pews became fashionable.

The small credence table set in the north wall of the sanctuary bears the arms of Kirkstall Abbey, three swords in fess, providing a direct link with the monks of the Abbey who originally built the church.

Some time ago a Bronze Age sword was found near the church. This is now on display in the Craven Museum, Skipton.

St. Mary-le-Gill to Thornton Church

Leave the churchyard and follow the path by the south churchyard wall down to go over Gill Syke and up onto the golf course. Cross the golf course directly to go through kissing-gate within the conifers.

Walk directly across the brow of the hill (the tower of Thornton Church now comes into view along with the Southern Yorkshire Dales. Over on the left Ingleborough, Malham and Pen-y-ghent dominate the skyline and behind us Pendle looms in the distance beyond Weets. To the right the moorland heights above Lothersdale display their ling-clad slopes) to go over fence-stile and on down to go over hedge-stile onto roadway. Cross the road and walk on to Thornton Church.

St. Mary's Church, Thornton

The embattled Perpendicular tower dominates the edifice, the south face of which bears an inscription and arms that I cannot make out along with a date, 1510. The inside of the church holds no hidden delights, but of interest is the churchyard draw well.

This octagonal structure bears the following

COLLARED URN
CORD & JABBED IMPRESSIONS
EARLY BRONZE AGE
FOUND IN A BARROW ON
HARE HILL, THORNTON-IN-
CRAVEN
CRAVEN MUSEUM
SKIPTON

inscription: "Qued Publicae Sanitati/bene vorat/H. Richardson Rector/Fontem hunc/Salutiferum et perantiquum/Tecto munivit/Anno AErae Christianae/MDCCLXIV (1764).

A Bronze Age collared urn displaying cord and jabbed impressions was found in a barrow on Hare Hill, Thornton-in-Craven. This is now on display in the Craven Museum, Skipton.

A fine Bronze Age bronze dagger was found in a field below the Manor House Residential Home, just up the road, in the 1960's (SD 909484).

Thornton Church to Earby Mines Museum

Pass over the stile opposite the churchyard gate and cross the field to go through gate, bear left to go over stile. Walk straight on to a gate at the corner of the road. From here, still in the field, bear right to go over stile in far fence. Keep on the same line to go over two stiles. Bear left across the field to go through stile below The Grange. Walk down the field on a right-diagonal to go over stile and on to go over wall-stile at Earby Church. Walk on to main road and cross into School Lane. The Earby Mines Museum is on the left after about 200 yards.

Earby Mines Museum

In the late 12th century, during the reign of King Stephen, Peter de Arthington gave lands in Earby for the founding of a Cluniac Priory. After the Dissolution the small nunnery, that had been maintained by various funds, reverted to the Crown and was later rented to Thomas Cranmer for 12 shillings a year.

After several transactions the nunnery became the property of Henry Mitchell and Robert Windle. Windle, a local man, took Holy Orders and became Rector of Tackley, Oxfordshire. On his death, Windle willed the lands of the nunnery to be sold for £440 to go towards building a grammar school in this part of West Craven. After a few legal difficulties a school was erected, and for three hundred years served the educational needs of Thornton and Earby.

After being superseded by more modern establishments it was occupied as a clinic by the West Riding County Council. It was later acquired by the Earby Mines Research Group who opened their museum here on 22nd May 1971.

On display inside this fine early 17th century building are many working model displays and material relating to lead mining in the Yorkshire Dales. Well worth a visit to gain an awareness of this once local industry.

Open April to October, 2pm to 9pm on Thursdays, and 2pm to 6pm on Sundays and Saturdays (Saturday, June to September).

Earby Mines Museum to The Red Lion

Take the road ahead between the factory buildings, continue along Water Street to branch left at the junction with the Lothersdale Road. Follow the lane up to Old Earby and the Red Lion.

Earby

Earby is graced by a romantic moorland stream that tumbles down from the hills, over waterfalls, to sing its song through the old village that shows much of a pre-industrial past. The Norman Survey mentions two 'Eurebi's', the other is taken to be Salterforth.

Man has settled here since ancient times: flint arrowheads and knives have been found on the surrounding moors, and two Bronze Age burial mounds testify to their passing. A 'Celtic' stone head was found some years ago in Wentcliff Beck, one of many discovered in West Craven. The beck once powered a corn mill that was established here in the 12th century. In a short while we shall walk up Mill Brow and along Mill Lane, now an overgrown hollow-way.

The Red Lion makes for a pleasant lunch or pint stop, good food and fine ale-a-plenty.

An excavation in the 1960's at the Rectory Allotment, Earby, yielded Bronze Age beaker sherds and pottery types, the finest being a long necked beaker with incised decoration, chevrons around the base, bands and diamonds around the top. A jet pulley lay with the beaker implying links with Whitby where most jet occurs.

Beneath this large stone cairn it was seen that a number of burials had taken place, the finds from which are now on display in the Craven Museum, Skipton.

The Red Lion to Kelbrook

Continue on along the road, past the Youth Hostel, to go through a gate set back on the right after about 200 yards. Follow the right-hand field boundary on, over stile and on to enter Mill Lane and on to the roadway. Cross the road to go over stile on left and on to go through metal gates. Follow line of left-hand fence on to go over stile at end of fields, then cross the next field bearing left past an old quarry to go over stile by gate.

Walk straight on, over a stream, and on to go over stile. Cross the field to go over stile, then over next field to go through gateway. Head over to the far right-hand corner to go over stile into overgrown lane. Walk on to Junction, left and walk on to next junction (we now no longer follow the 'Pendle Way' signs). Right, and follow the road down to Kelbrook and on to the village church.

Kelbrook

Recorded in the Norman Survey as 'Chelbroc' (Cenla's Brook), Kelbrook was at that time held by Ulf of Long Preston, having here six bovates of land (a bovate is a tax assessment of land, equivalent to about 20 acres).

Up until the 18th century the township was never more than a collection of farmsteads, Harden, Thisk Bank and Hague being principal. After which a hamlet grew around Dotcliffe Lane and the lower Harden Beck, farmworkers supplementing their income with handloom weaving of Worsted cloth.

By 1851 the community was one of some 900 persons with about a third being handloom weavers, with the rest being involved in farming and quarrying stone.

A wool spinning mill was built in the early 19th century being driven by a water wheel. By 1860 a power-loom weaving shed was added and both wool and cotton cloths produced. Textile manufacture ended in Kelbrook in the great fire of 1959 at Dotcliffe Mill with the work being transferred to Spring Mill, Earby.

Today the residents of Kelbrook travel out of the village each day to their work in the nearby townships. Most of the older houses are to be found on Dotcliffe Lane with Harden Brook forming the central feature.

The Craven Heifer, once a wayside inn and farm, provides a good lunchtime stop, serving a good selection of beers and meals at reasonable prices.

Ancient finds in the area are few, the best being a number of Neolithic flints found on Kelbrook Moor, and a fine stone 'Celtic' head at the Hague. The flints can be viewed in the Craven Museum, Skipton.

Like Earby, a hillside stream works its way down to ripple through this old Domesday settlement of 'Cheuebroc', and again its 18th century past is easily identified.

The oldest houses in the district are the Hagues: Great Hague has a datestone on the barn, H.R. M.R. 1707, the house being of a 17th century date. Middle Hague is dated 1618 with the initials I.H.E. above a three-arched doorhead. The Hague is somewhat later, but found in the grounds of the house was a 'Celtic' stone head, locally known as Kelbrook's oldest resident. The 'Old Slaughter House', by Low Bridge, has a datestone I:M:S:I 1682.

Up from the church stands the Craven Heifer, another chance for a quick pint or bite to eat.

Kelbrook to Anchor Inn, Salterforth

Walk up the track to the right of the Craven Heifer and on round to go over stile. Follow right-hand fence on to go down and over the line of the old railway to go over stile. Walk on to go over fence-stile on left and follow fence on, over footbridge and on, following path to go through small gate. Follow brookside path on to the roadway at Salterforth. Cross the main road and walk on to go left at the crossroads up to the Anchor Inn.

Salterforth

Salterforth is a tiny roadside hamlet, the old 17th century settlement is located around Cross Lane on the eastern side of the roadway. In former times Salterforth (Salters Ford) had a 'salt pie', that is to say that it was a salt storage and distribution point for the area.

The hamlet is sited on an ancient 'Salter's Way', one of a number of trans-Pennine routes that ran from the salterns of Northwich, Middlewich and

Nantwich, via Manchester into East Lancashire and West Yorkshire. The saltways were developed from pre-Conquest trackways and reached their greatest use in the 16th and 17th centuries.

My own investigations into this mediaeval industry has revealed an extraordinary transport network of tracks, roads, bridges, selling locations and stopping places, a study worthy of a book in itself.

The Anchor Inn stands aside the Leeds and Liverpool Canal and is a favourite lunch and evening meal stop for walkers and water folk alike. Good beer and very reasonably priced meals make for a place that you will visit time and time again.

Anchor Inn to Letcliff Park

Walk over the canal bridge and walk up the first farm lane on the right, past the cottage and on to go over stile by gate. Cross the field directly to go through wall-stile. Walk up the hill on a slight left-diagonal to corner of wall, and follow it on up to go over corner wall-stile. Follow right-hand wall on to go through wall-stile on right. Walk on to far left wall and follow it round to go through wall-stile. Cross the field directly into walled trackway and on to go over stile on the right of the 17th century Dye House Farm.

Walk on to go over fence-stile and follow right-hand wall up to enter top field. Follow hollow-way on to go through stile by gate. Walk on and around the far wall corner to go over stile by gate. Walk up the hill to go over stile on left. Cross the field, veering right to the viewing point above the park. From here fine views are gained over Craven and the southern Yorkshire Dales.

Letcliff Park to Bancroft Mill

Walk back into the summit picnic area and walk over to the right to leave the park area and onto the roadway. Right, and walk along the road to go left at junction on to Bancroft Mill.

Bancroft Mill

Bancroft Mill was the last cotton weaving mill to be established in Barnoldswick, in 1922. When the mill closed in 1978 it was largely demolished, apart from the engine house and chimney.

The steam engine — horizontal cross-compound condensing, 600 h.p., 16ft flywheel, 13 cotton ropes to second motion shaft, was built in 1915 by William Roberts and Sons, Nelson, Lancashire. This is all housed in original buildings with a coal-fired boiler.

It is open to the public Easter to October and regular steamings are held. For dates and further details contact Mr. W. Fisher on Earby (0282) 842214.

Bancroft Mill to Cross Keys Inn, Barnoldswick

Turn left at the entrance, cross the road and take the cobbled footpath on the right which will take you on down the 'Forty Steps' and on through Ouzeldale Wood to the roadway at the bottom. Right and walk on into the centre of Barnoldswick and the Cross Keys.

A visit to the Information Centre, located in the old library on Fernlea Road, is worth a visit. Displays on the area's historical development, details of local walks and town trails are all available here.

OTHER WALKING BOOKS
BY JOHN DIXON

'HISTORIC WALKS IN THE RIBBLE VALLEY'
1987. Dalesman.

'HISTORIC WALKS AROUND PENDLE'
1988. Dalesman.

'HISTORIC WALKS AROUND BLEASDALE
1988. Carnegie Press.

'HISTORIC WALKS AROUND RIBCHESTER'
1988. Carnegie Press.

'HISTORIC WALKS AROUND THE WEST PENNINE MOORS'
1988. Carnegie Press.

'HISTORIC WALKS AROUND THE FOREST OF BOWLAND'
1989. Carnegie Press.

'THE LEEDS & LIVERPOOL CANAL' — A HISTORY & GUIDE
1990. Carnegie Press.

'HISTORIC WALKS AROUND THE PENDLE WAY'
1990. Aussteiger Publications.

'WALK & DISCOVER THE RIBBLE VALLEY'
1990. Ribble Valley Borough.

'WALK & DISCOVER WHALLEY VILLAGE
1990. Ribble Valley Borough.